ANGEL™

Heroes &
Guardian Angels

TITAN

WWW.TITAN-COMICS.COM

Angel
The Official Collection Volume One
ISBN: 9781782763680

Published by Titan
A division of Titan Publishing Group Ltd.,
144 Southwark Street,
London
SE1 0UP.

Collecting material previously published in the
Official Buffy the Vampire Slayer Magazine and
the Official Angel Magazine, 1997-2007.

First Edition December 2015
10 9 8 7 6 5 4 3 2 1

Printed in China.
Titan.

Editor Natalie Clubb
Design Donna Askem
Senior Art Editor Rob Farmer
Contributing Editor Martin Eden

Art Director Oz Browne
Acting Studio Manager Selina Juneja
Publishing Manager Darryl Tothill
Publishing Director Chris Teather
Operations Director Leigh Baulch
Executive Director Vivian Cheung
Publisher Nick Landau

Acknowledgments
Titan Would Like to Thank...
The cast and crew of *Buffy* for giving up their
time to be interviewed, and Josh Izzo and Nicole
Spiegel at Fox for all their help in putting this
volume together.

ANGEL

THE CITY OF
ANGELS...

"Come on over to our offices and you'll see that there are still heroes in the world."

And so started Angel's new quest for redemption — helping the helpless in Los Angeles. Leaving behind his centuries of bloodlust as the notorious Angelus, the souled vampire continued his quest by becoming a beacon of hope for the most hopeless in their moment of need.

From humble beginnings as a PI to head of a global corporation, Angel proved his worth as a hero time and time again. And when the path ahead was unclear, he had his trusted friends to help him — determined to keep their friend — and hero — on the right track, at all costs.

In this first special collection we celebrate the journey of Angel and the friends and allies he made along the way.

ANGEL

Interviews

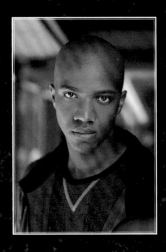

Profiles

CONTENTS

Features

THE A to Z OF

ANGEL

FANCY A QUICK REFRESHER COURSE ON FIVE YEARS OF THE SHOW? WELL LOOK NO FURTHER, AS WE PRESENT THE A-Z OF ANGEL – FROM ANGEL/ANGELUS TO, ER, ZEALOT HIGH PRIEST

WRITTEN BY KATE ANDERSON

A is for... ANGEL

Formerly an Irish commoner called Liam, sired by Darla. Together, the two of them terrorized, tortured and murdered anyone unfortunate enough to cross their path. Angel was cursed by a gypsy tribe after killing one of their clan. They restored his soul, forcing him to live in anguish over his evil acts. After falling in love with the Slayer, the brooding vampire left Buffy and Sunnydale to fight evil in L.A., where he continues to seek redemption and forgiveness for his heinous acts.

AND ALSO...

ANGELUS: The name of Angel's evil alter ego when he's without a soul. A moment of true happiness will result in Angel turning evil.

C is for... CORDELIA

Once Sunnydale High School's Miss Popular and a member of the Scooby Gang. Cordelia moved to L.A. to pursue her acting aspirations and ended up working for Angel Investigations. Helping the helpless was a life-changing experience for the acid-tongued Cordy, particularly when Doyle passed on his mind-splitting visions to her. Cordelia and Angel's deep friendship eventually turned into love. But alas, it wasn't to be. After giving birth to the evil that was Jasmine, Cordelia lapsed into a coma. But before passing away, Cordelia returned to help the man she loved; using her last gift from The Powers That Be, she became Angel's guardian angel.

AND, LET'S NOT FORGET...

CONNOR: Now known as Stephen, Angel and Darla's son had a dysfunctional relationship with Angel. Snatched as a baby by Holtz, Connor grew up in a Hell dimension believing the vampire hunter to be his father. He eventually returned to L.A., seeking revenge against his real father, whom he despised. But in a final act of love for his son, Angel struck a deal with Wolfram & Hart in order for Connor to have a normal family life. However, he did return to fight alongside Angel one last time.

D is for... DOYLE

Allen Francis Doyle was a half-human Bracken demon. He was an invaluable member of Angel Investigations, largely due to the visions of the future he received from The Powers That Be. Always the reluctant hero, Doyle sacrificed himself to deactivate a deadly device that had the power to wipe out impure demons.

E is for... EVIL LAW-FIRM, WOLFRAM & HART

W&H specialize in representing demons. Employees included Hamilton, the mysterious henchman of Wolfram & Hart's Senior Partners; Holland Manners, the former Vice President of Special Projects who met a rather nasty end at Darla and Drusilla's hands; and Knox, the geeky lab assistant/follower of Illyria.

EVE: When Angel took charge of the L.A. branch of Wolfram & Hart, Eve was the liaison between W&H's Senior Partners and Angel. Eve was in cahoots (and in bed) with Angel's nemesis, Lindsey McDonald.

B is for... BIG BADS

Angel and co. have had to face off against some unforgettable Big Bads in their time. They didn't come any more intimidating than The Beast; an enormous rocky demon, summoned from beneath the ground. A seemingly indestructible killing machine, The Beast was sent to bring about the Apocalypse. Although certainly not as imposing, vampire hunter Daniel Holtz was also a nasty individual. Obsessed with destroying Angel and Darla after they murdered his family and made his daughter one of their own kind, Holtz got his own back by kidnapping Angel's son, Connor. Holtz was in league with SahJhan, a time-traveling demon and member of a violent demon race that thrived on chaos. SahJhan made a deal with Holtz and turned the vampire hunter into stone for over 200 years so he could get revenge in the future. As prophesied, Connor destroyed SahJhan.

F is for... FRED

Fred became an important member of the team after they rescued her from Pylea. A brilliant mathematician and physicist, when Angel took over Wolfram &Hart, she became head of the science division. She dated Gunn for a while, oblivious to Wesley's affections. Fred and Wes finally got together but she got infected by a parasitic demon. The sweet, kind and quirky Fred everyone knew and loved was, alas, no more.

G is for... GUNN

The leader of a gang of street fighters, Charles Gunn was a sort of urban Robin Hood figure. The self-appointed vampire slayer and demon hunter continued to fight the good fight when he joined Angel Investigations. Often the brawn of the group rather than the brains, when Angel took charge of W&H, that all changed. Gunn underwent a procedure to enhance his mind with a comprehensive knowledge of the law. The transformation even included ditching his comfy casuals for smart and snappy business suits!

H is for... HARMONY

A popular girl in high school, Harmony got to stay young and beautiful forever when she was turned into a vampire during her graduation. She had a brief relationship with Spike until he turned his affections towards a certain Slayer. When Angel took over Wolfram & Hart, Harmony became his secretary – sorry, personal assistant.

I is for... ILLYRIA

An ancient demon, able to gestate in its human host, killing and destroying their body and soul in the process. Fred was the unfortunate recipient of the ancient demon's parasitic essence.

J is for... JASMINE

Unexpected offspring after Cordelia's tumble in the sack with Connor. Mass brainwasher Jasmine was a Goddess from another dimension who had the ability to control the hearts and minds of those she encountered. A beautiful woman on the surface, but in reality Jasmine was nothing more than a maggot-ridden manifestation!

K is for... KATE

Former L.A.P.D. detective and an invaluable ally to Angel. After discovering Angel's true identity – not to mention the murder of her father at the hands of a vampire – Kate developed an intense hatred towards Angel and became obsessed with ridding the city of "his kind". After Angel saved her from taking her own life, she renounced her vendetta against him.

L is for... LORNE

Otherwise known as Krevlornswath of the Deathwok Clan or The Host. A green-skinned karaoke-loving demon with a snappy dress sense and an extravagant persona to match. Lorne has the ability to predict the future by reading people's auras while they sing. He became the head of Wolfram & Hart's entertainment division when Angel took over; a role which he took to like a duck to water.

M is for... MORGAN & MCDONALD

LILAH MORGAN: Former ruthlessly ambitious Wolfram & Hart employee. It was Lilah's job to keep tabs on Angel and generally make life difficult for the vampire. She struck up an intense and  passionate relationship with Wesley. Even death couldn't stop Lilah: she came back to show Angel how to run a successful evil law-firm.

LINDSEY MCDONALD: Formerly one of Wolfram & Hart's rising stars, and a constant thorn in Angel's side. When Angel was put in charge of W&H, Lindsey returned, seeking revenge against his nemesis and the Senior Partners. He was killed by Lorne, of all people – which didn't go down well with Lindsey!

N is for... NINA

Bitten by a werewolf, Nina struggled to come to terms with her life-changing situation. Angel helped her to adjust to her new life, and she developed romantic intentions towards the hunky vampire.

O is for... ORACLES

One of the channels through which The Powers That Be communicate with lesser beings. They offered guidance for Angel towards his prophetic destiny. Ultimately killed by Vocah.

P is for... PLENTY...

THE POWERS THAT BE: A mysterious and powerful force intent on making things right. **AND**

PYLEA: Alternative demon dimension where Lorne comes from; home to a variety of different species.
AND ALSO...

PHANTOM DENNIS: Cordelia's resident ghost roommate.

Q is for... QUOR'TOTH

Horrible Hell dimension where Connor grew up.

R is for... RUSSELL WINTERS

Rich and powerful vampire and a client of Wolfram & Hart. The first villain to appear on Angel, he met a grisly end when Angel sent him flying out of a high-rise window – in daylight.

S is for... SPIKE

Also known as William the Bloody, he once wreaked havoc wherever he went, along with Angelus, Darla and Drusilla.. Spike was responsible for the deaths of two Slayers, but eventually fell in love with one. After earning his soul, Spike sacrificed himself to close the Hellmouth. He then materialized in the offices of Wolfram & Hart..

SKIP: A demon working for The Powers That Be. Skip was responsible for demonizing Cordelia and enabling her to keep her visions. He also tried, unsuccessfully, to further Jasmine's coming and fought with Angel and the gang.

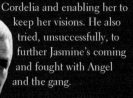

SHANSHU PROPHECY: A prophecy relating to a vampire with a soul fulfilling his destiny as a champion to become human again.

T is for... THE GROOSALUGG

A half-human warrior who became the new ruler of Pylea, when Princess Cordelia abolished the former racist government. So smitten with his Princess, the Groosalugg followed Cordelia back to L.A. But eventually Groo realized that Cordy didn't return his affections, and was in love with an altogether different champion...

U is for... UNREQUITED LOVE

Love makes the world go round, and the *Angel*verse is no exception, particularly when it comes to unrequited love. Doyle had a massive crush on Cordelia, and they shared a powerful kiss before he died. Angel has had his share of admirers, including Fred and Kate Lockley. Groo and Cordelia made a cute couple, but Groo soon realized that Cordy was in love with Angel. Lindsey McDonald was rather taken with a certain blonde vampire – and no, we don't mean Spike! Wesley's heart belonged to Fred, who was never short of admirers herself. Knox had a soft spot for Fred although the attraction was never returned. And then there was the whole Connor/Cordelia/Angel love triangle – but the less said about that the better!

V is for... VAMPS

Former prostitute-turned vampire, Darla had a relationship with Angel spanning more than 150 years. But when Angel was cursed with a soul, she abandoned him when he needed her most. W&H resurrected her, but she ultimately killed herself so that her son could be born. Drusilla was sired by Angelus, and became Spike's long-time love, not to mention as nutty as a fruitcake. W&H brought Dru to L.A. to turn Darla back into one of the undead, and they went on a killing spree together.

W is for... WESLEY

The former bumbling Watcher was a self-styled rogue demon hunter before joining Angel Investigations. He quickly found his place within the team, becoming the resident researcher, thanks to his demon knowledge and ability to translate ancient languages. A competent leader, Wesley was a good stand-in for Angel as head of Angel Investigations. Not particularly successful with the ladies, Wesley did manage to find true love in the end with Fred. But their happiness, at least in this world, was short-lived.

X is for... X-CELLENT TV

Which sums *Angel* up perfectly!

Y is for... Y OH WHY!

'Y' did it have to end???! Cut short in its prime by The WB, *Angel* had at least two years' worth of excellent television left in it.

Z is for... ZEALOTS

The High Priest Zealots in the Jasmine episodes. Hey, what else is there for 'Z'??!

SEASON 1

"City Of"

First US airdate
5 October 1999

First UK airdate
5 January 2000

Synopsis

Having upped stakes – sorry, sticks – to L.A., our favorite member of the undead gets a visit from a guy called Doyle. Doyle is half-demon (on his father's side) and explains to Angel that he's been sent by 'The Powers That Be' to help him fight evil, save the helpless, rescue the innocent and all that.

Angel's first 'mission' is to protect a girl called Tina who's a waitress and aspiring movie star. Angel makes contact with her by pretending to chat her up. He senses her loneliness and they get talking. Tina invites him to a party and, surprise, surprise, Angel bumps into Cordelia Chase – who has moved to L.A. to pursue an acting career. After the party, Angel unfortunately reveals his true face to a petrified Tina. She flees only to find another vampire waiting for her back at her apartment – a man Tina has been running from – Russell Winters, a rich, powerful, well-connected vampire who just so happens to be feeling a bit peckish. When Angel returns to Tina's apartment, he discovers her body and vows to track down the people responsible for her death. Meanwhile, Russell Winters prepares to move on to his next victim – Cordelia...

Actor Info

Glenn Quinn:

Glenn Martin Christopher Francis Quinn (phew!) was born on 28 May in Dublin, Ireland. He moved to the United States in 1988 and got his first break playing a pool shark in a Richard Marx video (for the single "Satisfied"). Glenn got to kiss actress Gwyneth Paltrow when he appeared in the movie *Shout* (1991) which also featured John Travolta. *Angel* aside, Glenn is probably best known for his role as Mark Healy in the hugely popular sitcom *Roseanne*. Glenn left *Angel* after nine episodes, but his character, Doyle, was a big hit with fans and attained something of a cult status. Most recently, Glenn starred alongside Majandra Delfino (Maria in *Roswell*) in the movie *R.S.V.P.*, a black comedy thriller.

Trivia

✝ **The first** draft of the shooting script featured the character of Whistler playing the part of Angel's mentor, rather than Doyle.

✝ **Angel** drives a rather cool black 1968 Plymouth Belvedere GTX convertible.

✝ **Both** Tracy Middendorf and Vyto Ruginis have had roles on *The X-Files*. Tracy popped up in "Signs and Wonders", while Vyto appeared in the episode "Medusa".

Memorable Dialog

Doyle (to homeless woman): "Get a job, you lazy sow!" +

Cordelia: "I finally get invited to a nice place with... no mirrors... and... lots of curtains... Hey, you're a vampire!" +

Statistics

No. of vamps dusted: 4

No. of times you actually feel sorry for Cordy: 4

No. of deaths: 1

No. of times Angel takes his shirt off: 2

Episode Credits

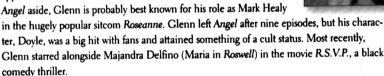

Written by	David Greenwalt & Joss Whedon	
Directed by	Joss Whedon	
Angel	David Boreanaz	
Cordelia Chase	Charisma Carpenter	
Allen Francis Doyle	Glenn Quinn	
Russell Winters	Vyto Ruginis	
Lindsey McDonald	Christian Kane	
Tina	Tracy Middendorf	
Stacy	Jon Ingrassia	
Margo	Renee Ridgeley	
Manager	Sam Pancake	
Janice	Gina McClain	

Compiled by Kate Anderson

WRITTEN BY TARA O'SHEA

DAVID'S
DISCUSSIONS

DAVID BOREANAZ PROVED A BIG HIT AT A RECENT *BUFFY/ANGEL* CONVENTION AND *ANGEL MAGAZINE* WAS THERE TO REPORT ON ALL THE HIGHLIGHTS! HERE, DAVID SHARES HIS THOUGHTS ON HIS FAVORITE *ANGEL* EPISODES, THE CANCELLATION OF THE SHOW, *ANGEL* TELE-MOVIES AND MUCH, MUCH MORE!

all it Wolfram & Hart's Chicago office. A group of *Angel* stars – including David Boreanaz – were just some of the guests who appeared recently in the Windy City at the Flashback Weekend, an annual *Buffy* and *Angel* fan event. Over the course of the weekend, David Boreanaz and his co-stars (including Christian Kane and Stephanie Romanov) thrilled fans – some of whom traveled to the convention from as far away as Yorkshire, and as close as the Chicago suburbs.

Sporting lightened locks and an easy smile as he takes to the stage in a rare US convention appearance, David first and foremost thanks the devoted fans of *Angel* for their support over the years. "A lot of the reasons why our show continued was because of fans like you," David starts, "and I really enjoyed the last five seasons of *Angel* and two-and-a-half seasons of *Buffy*. I'm happy we got the opportunity to give you guys some great stories," David says as he leads the excited crowd in a round of applause.

David admits that it's difficult for him to pin down which episodes, over the course of the

series, were his favorites. However, he soon manages to decide on the series premiere "City of", written and directed by series creator Joss Whedon. "It was a challenge to separate myself from *Buffy* and prove that I could take a [new] show on," he says. "We really didn't know what we were doing for the 12 days it took to shoot ['City of']. We did a lot of things wrong, but through that we learned."

Another favorite was the second season's "Are You Now Or Have You Ever Been", due in large part to the period setting. "That's one of my favorite episodes, just because of the time and the clothing," David reveals. "We shot up at Griffith Observatory. There's a James Dean statue there. It was cool, just hanging out with the crew and overlooking the cityscape. There's so many episodes that I have enjoyed. It's hard. I do an episode and literally space out, and for me it's

really what's going on in the next episode. So now that they're all done, maybe one day I'll sit down with [my son] Jaden and I'll watch them and he'll ask me things about them. And that's when I'll really have a chance to look at them again.

"*Angel* for me was a very emotional five years," David reflects. "In the first season of *Buffy*, [Angel] was just kind of like a recurring character. Then he just kind of evolved. And holding a show down is very difficult. It's a lot of pressure on your shoulders, and you're in pretty much every scene. You really run that gamut of continuously changing and challenging that character so it doesn't become boring. And the writers allowed me to do that. So it was much harder walking away from *Angel*.

One missed opportunity that David does regreat is further development of the tempestuous relationship between Angel

and fellow souled vamp – and fellow Buffy beau – Spike. "I think a better, more [involved] relationship with James [Marsters] and I – the whole Spike and Angel thing – would have been fun. I think that by the end of this season, you see these two characters pretty much doing 'Who's on first?' in a way. It's really just so sad. They are just the saddest group of characters. They try so hard, and they can't grasp it. But they're so macho and cool. I would really have loved to have seen more development towards that [relationship]. I had this one episode that I pitched which would have been really funny, and it's almost the kind of *Some Like it Hot* thing, where James and I had to actually dress up as women. It would have been cool. I can walk in a pair of heels!"

DAVID'S SOUL

Fellow convention guests, Christian (Lindsey) Kane and Stephanie (Lilah) Romanov, have nothing but praise for the series star, particularly David's skills as a first-time director in "Soul Purpose."

"I worked with David for years [as an actor]," Christian notes of the episode, "and all of a sudden I walked on [to the set] and he was a director. He was unbelievable, and he was such a pleasure, and I think it was probably one of the better episodes. It was one of my favorite episodes I was a part of."

"Everyone was so surprised at how organized he was," Stephanie adds. "How good of a job he did. He didn't seem like someone who had never directed before. Everybody was very impressed."

"It was a fun experience," David says of his directorial debut. "Something that I looked at as a big challenge to take on. I'd always wanted to get in the director's chair, and the cast made it very easy for me. I think my perspective on it was just to allow them to do what they wanted to do. I think they know what we're doing. I had a really good time operating the camera. I did some shots, and I had a good time. Is directing in my future? I think so, because I enjoyed it. It was something that I loved to do, and I had fun doing it. So it's not something that I immediately want to jump back into, but I know that someday I probably will."

"It's his show," says Christian, "so he worked his ass off. We just show up two or three days a week and work our asses off, but David's there every day," actor Christian Kane explains. "And literally, we're in a union as an actor and they have us for 12 hours, no matter what, and most of the time David shows up and he's there for 12 hours every day. If he goes to work at 9, he's there 'til 9. If he goes to work at 5:30 in the morning, then he's there 'til 5:30 [in the evening]. And this is on a good day. Other days, you go two, three hours longer."

become a tight group. I wouldn't be here without actors like Stephanie and Christian," David notes, sincerely. "Alexis, Amy, Andy, J. The people that were in every scene with us – that's the show. I know it's called *Angel*, but Angel is about redemption. It's about the characters around him, and that represents everybody who's on it. It's not one person. It's a whole. I keep stressing that because that's who I am, that's how I wanted to run the show. It's about the people that are involved."

David admits that filming the final episodes was emotional for the entire cast. "We shot one of the scenes, I think in Episode 21 with the whole group of people, talking in a circle. There was a moment where I got emotional. I was looking at every one of these characters in the face, and explaining to them what we have to do and how we have to fight, it was kind of ironic how – you know, don't let the network change the storyline. Continue to stay for it, even though they decided not to pick us up, and not come back. We stayed true to who we were, and we went out the way we wanted to go out.

"It was hard," he says, of filming the final scene of the series finale. "Amy [Acker] was crying a lot. The tears were flowing. When you work on a show for that long a period of time, you know a lot about each other. You become a family. And it was tough. It was hard. I kept fighting it. We ended up shooting in an alleyway, and we'd kind of started the show in an alleyway. And some amazing things

Season Five also featured closure – of a sort – to the Buffy and Angel romance in the form of "The Girl In Question". Spike and Angel journey to Italy where Buffy is reported to be in the clutches of The Immortal. "In Episode 20, we went to Italy, and it was a good way for the two of us to go out. I don't think that Buffy and Angel's relationship is necessarily over. I don't think that in Joss' world that there really is a dying character. I think he really is a genius who has the opportunity to bring those characters back. But I think that [Buffy and Angel have] gone on different paths."

David notes that the original finale arc plans really did not change after the cancellation news broke. "I think that's what's great about Joss [Whedon] and David [Greenwalt] – this the way it would have ended, with maybe a few minor adjustments. I think they stood strong to their conditions and we went out saying that this is really about redemption, this show. And your fight for redemption. That's what Angel's character is about. That's pretty much what happens in one sense. But they weren't going to change much of anything."

David is quick to point out *Angel* was an ensemble effort. "Working with the whole cast was great for those five seasons," he says. "It can take a long time to shoot a specific scene – you get your master shots, and do your close-ups – so by the end you're just kind of exhausted and you

> "*ANGEL* FOR ME WAS A VERY EMOTIONAL FIVE YEARS. IT'S A LOT OF PRESSURE ON YOUR SHOULDERS. YOU REALLY RUN THAT GAMUT OF CONTINUOUSLY CHANGING AND CHALLENGING THAT CHARACTER SO IT DOESN'T BECOME BORING. IT WAS MUCH [HARDER] WALKING AWAY FROM *ANGEL*."

DAVID ON CONNOR

David has plenty of praise for Vincent Kartheiser, who joined the series in Season Three as the adult Connor.

"They tested him, and we did a scene and I felt his energy was pretty much right on the character. As the character progressed, I think there were some difficulties in dealing with [the storyline.] He's now 16, he's now an adolescent, and how does that relationship really work with Angel? And it kinda felt like a little bit that he lost some things there. I think the writers didn't maintain the strength of that character. But what he did was great, and as far as the character connection with him, it was a pleasure. He was a baby, now he's 16. I mean, where do you go from there? It's pretty weird!"

happen in that alleyway. And Kelly Manners, who was the producer of the show, and I, we both cried. It was very emotional. I'm really proud of the way they ended it. It was very emotional. It was tight.

"When we shot the last scene, my father was there. It was great to have my dad there. It was 4:30 in the morning. We were shooting in an alley, we were using a rain machine. It was very cool. So we were soaking wet. Drenched. It was a nightmare, just like the way we started the damn show! And I said goodbye to everybody. Hugged the producer. Kelly cried, and my dad and I walked down the alley. That was the last thing. It was great to have my father there. He's a very important person in my life. Someone who I respect, and think highly

of. He's my best friend. Someone you can talk to about anything. I'm very fortunate to have him."

David has not really thought about whether or not he would like his two-year-old son, Jaden, to eventually follow in his footsteps and become an actor. "I want

him to get grass stains on his knees. I want him to be a kid. I really love that. My parents never forced anything on me. I'm not going to push him in that direction. Whatever Jaden decides he wants to do when he gets to that age, being responsible and making choices, I'm there for him for whatever he wants to do. I'm not going to say, 'And now you will start your classical training.' I honestly don't subscribe to that. Some actors do, and I just think it's a lot of [rubbish]. Look, I'm not a Shakespearean trained actor. I didn't go to get classically trained, and I'm saying that's a bad thing. I respect that highly, and I've read Shakespeare, and Chekov, and that stuff is interesting to me. I just think life is a great experience. Going out

REMEMBERING GLENN QUINN

One of Season Five's arcs included Lindsey pretending to be Doyle – the character created by original *Angel* series castmember Glenn Quinn who passed away in December 2002. Some of the scenes proved difficult for Christian and David both of whom were close to Glenn. David shares his thoughts.

"That was hard. That was very difficult. I really kind of keep Glenn at a distance, and that's something that to me was very painful to go through because he was a very strong person in my life when the show started. For me, he represented someone who taught me a lot about acting, as a person. Glenn was a great guy. When you have situations like that, you kind of use it for the scene. I remember [*Angel* producer] Kelly Manners taught me that. To use it. When the moment came, I didn't want to do it, and Kelly said, 'Well, just use what you're feeling in the scene.' Glenn, God bless his soul, he's in a great place and I love him. He's looking down and drinking Guinness and smiling at me."

in different cities and different places and seeing people. I've come to Chicago, and now I've got a handful of characters I can play. This is exciting."

After eight years playing an undead brooding vampire hunk, David is philosophical about being typecast. "If I was so concerned being recognized just as Angel I think that I would have stopped playing this character a long time ago. I never look at it as a crutch. I look at it as a great experience and something I've learned from. I think all actors are going to play a role and take that [experience] with them, whoever they are, and just continue to grow as a person. If I am overly obsessive about it I think that would work negatively against me. I embrace it and I loved it, and I continue to grow and challenge myself. That's where you create challenges.

"And as far as getting involved with another television series [someday] – it's a lot of work. It's a lot of time, it's a lot of effort. So I'm just taking a little break from that right now. But I'm open to TV, theater, film. I love to act. I love to challenge myself. I love people saying, 'You can't do that' because that's a big

challenge. That's what fuels me. If I don't grasp that, then I'd be so obsessed about that. So that's the way I've used that.

"I'm in an interesting spot in my career right now – in my life. There's a big transition going on. It's exciting because I have the opportunity to kind of not be so closed into fitting in a project in a hiatus where I have two months left to do something – which is very hard to do, because it took nine months to shoot the show. So in a way it's bittersweet for me that [*Angel*'s cancellation] is opening up other roles and it's challenging for me as an actor. It's horrible for the fans, because you guys are great and we would love to tell more stories for you of course. At the same time it's just that give-and-take kind of period. But there is a big side of me that nobody knows and I'm excited to share that with all of you in the future. That [side of me] is really kind of silly, stupid, giddy. Kind of off-the-cuff. I'm really not that broody a person."

Following the series' cancellation, The WB issued a statement regarding the possibility of *Angel* movies-of-the-week to wrap up the storylines. However, as excited as long-time fans are by the idea of the characters continuing – albeit in telefilms and not a weekly series – David has been open about his lack of desire to revisit the character on the small screen.

"I'll be honest – I don't see myself going back to doing an *Angel* television movie with these characters. I would like to see a film be done. I think a big screen version would be fantastic. I think that the way they shot *Angel*, and the scope of it, how large it is, and it's shot in Los Angeles, and the effects that we did, and what we did in eight days – if we had two or three months, we could really blow some sh*t out of the water. I say that of the characters. It would be really cool to bring that on, and I would like to do that. That would be an extremely great challenge."

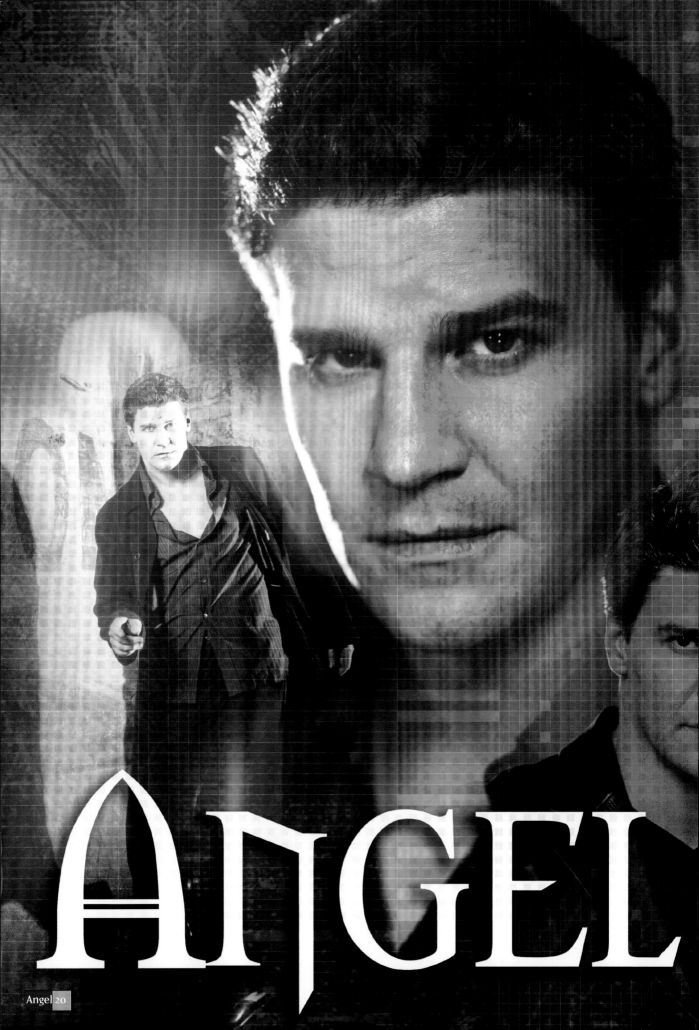

ANGEL CASE FILES:

THUMBNAIL BIO:

Sired by Darla in 1753, he had a long, murderous career as Angelus until a gypsy curse restored his soul and his conscience in 1898. Except for a couple of brief stints as Angelus, he's been a good guy ever since. He came to Sunnydale in 1996 to watch over the Slayer, Buffy, the love of his life, and moved to LA four years later to make his own life as a champion of good for the Powers That Be, became head of Angel Investigations, and father – with Darla, of all people! – of miracle baby Connor.

BEST KNOWN FOR:

Brooding. Nobody broods better than the Big Guy; he's so good at it that even when he's only doing laundry in the basement, his friends all assume he's down there to brood.

FUNNIEST MOMENT:

Angel realises that riding on the passenger seat of Wesley's motorcycle also means wearing the passenger helmet – which is pink ("First Impressions").

NEVER ASK HIM TO:

Sing. Anything. Especially Barry Manilow. His duet with Connor, singing "Jasmine" to the tune of "Mandy" is so funny it hurts ("The Magic Bullet").

BRAINIEST MOMENT:

Playing a museum guide ("She"). To escape the notice of the museum security guards, Angel steps up to a Manet and wows the guests with an insider's commentary on the painter and his friends, including a hint that the writer Baudelaire knew a real vampire.

SCARIEST MOMENT:

Locking up Holland Manners and his guests with Darla and Drusilla ("Reunion"). You'd expect Angelus to reject Holland's plea for protection from vampires – but it's Angel who turns his back.

WORST MOMENT:

Connor locks Angel in a metal box and sinks him in the sea, where he can neither escape nor drown ("Tomorrow").

WHAT MATTERS MOST:

Buffy, Cordelia and, mostly, Connor. In "Peace Out", the High Priest tells Angel he's fighting only for Connor's sake; in "Home", Angel accepts Wolfram & Hart's offer, even though he considers it a deal with the devil, entirely because W&H can give Connor a different life.

MOMENT OF PERFECT HAPPINESS:

Angel makes love to Buffy for the first time (*Buffy*; "Surprise)". Unfortunately, this sets off the gypsy curse, strips him of his soul and turns him into Angelus. Bye-bye happiness!

MOMENT OF PERFECT HAPPINESS, II:

When a demon's blood makes Angel human, he makes love to Buffy and discovers the blissful pairing of peanut butter and chocolate. It doesn't get any better than this – until Angel goes all broody and noble, and sacrifices his happiness so that he can remain a champion ("I Will Remember You").

MOMENT OF TRUTH:

Angel vs. Angelus ("Orpheus"). In a drug-induced hallucination (or is it more than hallucination?) the champion and the vampire revisit Angel's good deeds, and go head to head over which of them is the alter ego. ✈

BY K. STODDARD HAYES

COSMIC GIRL

By Rod Edgar

TELEVISION CHARACTERS DON'T OFTEN COME AS COMPLEX OR INTERESTING AS CORDELIA CHASE – SHE HAS CERTAINLY EXPERIENCED MANY CHANGES DURING HER SIX-YEAR *BUFFY/ANGEL* JOURNEY. WE CAUGHT UP WITH CHARISMA CARPENTER FOR A RARE, EXCLUSIVE INTERVIEW ABOUT HER – AND CORDY'S – PAST, PRESENT AND FUTURE.

It's been an incredible evolution for Cordelia Chase – from stuck-up High School snob to compassionate, courageous heroine, right up (literally) to higher being. While playing the complex character, actress Charisma Carpenter has also undergone a dramatic journey. After three seasons on *Buffy* she left the popular, established series to take a starring role alongside David Boreanaz in spin-off series *Angel*.

Angel's third season saw the biggest changes yet for Cordelia – becoming part-demon to retain her precognitive powers, enjoying a romance with other-worldly hero the Groosalugg, and finally realizing her true feelings for vampire detective Angel by helping him through the loss and return of his son. In a dramatic cliffhanger, the Season Three finale concluded with Cordelia's new demon powers forcing her to ascend beyond the mortal plane before she had the chance to declare her newly discovered love.

We caught up with Charisma as she was preparing to return for the show's fourth season – still digesting the recent dramatic events and considering what lies ahead for Cordelia.

It's called a cliffhanger, a season-ender, so
a lot of people were a little confused as to
the way it ended and my ascension, and
"does that mean that I'm not coming
back next year?", and all of that. I thought
it was appropriate, I guess. I'm curious to
find out what's next for Cordelia as far as,
when she has her powers, where are they
going to go with that now? Like, am I
going to come back, and when I come
back will I still have my powers? Giving
her all this power – I don't know what
we're going to do with that, so we'll see.

Angel and I being together. So it's been
my understanding that the minute you
put two leads together on a show nobody
wants to watch anymore, and it becomes
tiresome and boring, or whatever. So I
think like any good drama there should
be conflict and Groo presented a great
deal of conflict – we couldn't act out
our feelings, or [Angel] couldn't. He
couldn't come right out and say it,
besides his other stilted emotional
problems. (Joke!)

YOU MENTIONED CONCERNS ABOUT
WHAT MIGHT HAPPEN IF TWO
LEADS GET TOGETHER – THE
MOONLIGHTING EFFECT. ARE YOU
CONCERNED ABOUT WHAT MIGHT
HAPPEN WITH AN ANGEL AND
CORDELIA ROMANCE?
A little bit. For me as an actress I would
want us to act out on it, because, I think,

> "I THINK IT'S IMPERATIVE
> FOR CHARACTERS TO CHANGE TO
> STAY WATCHABLE. THEY HAVE TO
> GROW AND HAVE CONFLICT, AND
> THROUGH CONFLICT IS GROWTH
> AND STRENGTH."

I was grateful because I was kind of bored
with Cordelia being hurt all the time and
in pain. I was over it.

Yeah, I like that. I think it is more heroic,
and I just think that too much power
though… I don't know how to explain it… I
don't think that it's as fun. There is one hero
on the show, and that is Angel, ultimately.

I thought it was necessary. I thought it
was necessary to tell the story because
the whole point of having Groo is that
he's an obstacle to get in the way of

you set it up – there's got to be a pay-off.
But I think that would be detrimental to
the series, if we did. So thank God those
sorts of decisions aren't in my hands. I
don't know what the right thing to do is.

OF COURSE, ANOTHER ELEMENT
THAT'S BEEN THROWN INTO THE
MIX THIS SEASON IS THE INTRO-
DUCTION OF ANGEL'S HOSTILE
TEENAGE SON, CONNOR. WHAT
SORT OF ROLE MIGHT CORDELIA
PLAY IN THAT RELATIONSHIP?
AN INTERMEDIARY?
Hopefully not mother. I think, though, that
is the direction it's going – Angel's the
father and I'm the mother. They often use
family as a metaphor for our union, the
group; the clan, the whole investigative
office, everybody that's part of the investiga-
tion service that we offer – we're all very
bonded together. We've been through a lot

together for whatever reason. We're family. I think that bringing in a child kind of makes us the matriarch and the patriarch and then our getting together, our feelings for each other, makes that even more solidified. And you know, I don't know how I feel about being presented as a maternal person on the show – I'd rather still kind of stay sassy and talkback, and be the wise-cracking, one-liner deliverer person.

THERE ARE CONSTANT DEVELOPMENTS ON THE SHOW, NOTHING SEEMS TO STAY THE SAME FOR VERY LONG, AND AS WE'VE SEEN WITH WESLEY, CHANGES HAPPEN TO THE MAIN CHARACTERS. DO THE CONSTANT CHANGES EVER UNNERVE YOU OR UNSETTLE YOU?

No, they've never unnerved me or unsettled me. I think it's imperative for characters to change to stay watchable. They have to grow and have conflict, and through conflict is growth and strength. That's what life is like, and any good story-teller would try to make their stories as lifelike and identifiable as possible.

IN ADDITION TO THE CHANGES THAT ARE GOING ON ONSCREEN, THERE HAVE BEEN PLENTY OF CHANGES BEHIND THE SCENES AS WELL. SHOWRUNNER DAVID GREENWALT IS LEAVING, AND EXECUTIVE PRODUCER TIM MINEAR WILL BE WORKING ON FIREFLY. WHAT SORT OF IMPACT DO YOU THINK THAT MIGHT HAVE ON THE SHOW?

I don't know. I don't know what kind of impact it's going to have. But Tim Minear and Joss are still an integral part of the writing crew. They did bring in new writers – it's the largest writing staff we've had. Hopefully the most talented. And there are some writers that will be staying with us, and some that had occasionally written for us but that were mainly on *Buffy* that are coming over from *Buffy* 100 per cent. So I've been reassured, and this is Joss' baby and life. I have extreme admiration for his work ethic, and I'm sure he will bring the right person in in place of David Greenwalt.

YOU ORIGINALLY AUDITIONED FOR THE ROLE OF BUFFY. DO YOU NOW FEEL THAT GETTING THE PART OF CORDELIA WAS FOR THE BEST?

Yeah. I think I'm better suited to Cordelia.

THE CHARACTER'S BEEN THROUGH AN INCREDIBLE TRANSFORMATION OVER THE YEARS. HAVE YOU FOUND IT DIFFICULT TO MAKE THAT TRANSITION FROM WHAT SHE WAS TO WHAT SHE'S BECOME?

No, I was begging for it.

DO YOU THINK THE TRANSFORMATION WAS A NATURAL EVOLUTION FOR THE CHARACTER, OR HOW MUCH DO YOU THINK WAS NECESSITATED BY THE MOVE TO ANGEL?

Well, it didn't happen right away on *Angel*. It happened for her, but the audience was privy to her change or her experience through being hungry and not getting jobs as an actress and having been defeated in that category. She was really going for being an actress and it wasn't working. It wasn't working out for her. So she has this silent suffering that the audience knew about, but she never let anybody else know about. And I think that was sort of the introduction of the change. Through pain is growth. I think that's when it started – the first few episodes of *Angel*. And I loved it. I wanted to be challenged. I wanted to have my character fleshed out and to become more three-dimensional, and become more of a human being. Not everybody is one personality type, even though we might think so. Obviously, even the nastiest of people have more to their personality than just that nastiness, and also there's a lot of reasons for why they're probably that way. So I think that over the years she's had the time, and she's had the screentime, to parlay that, and make that happen, and have that show up and written about.

DO YOU FEEL THE ORIGINAL ESSENCE OF THE CHARACTER STILL REMAINS? IS SHE STILL TRUE TO WHO SHE ORIGINATED FROM?

No, I don't think that the way she was initially written is anything like what she is like now, at all.

Of course! I was very scared! I was flattered to be given the opportunity to star with David, and there was only going to be three of us, initially, so there would be a lot more screentime to develop her character. And they told me, they gave me hints about what lay ahead for Cordelia, and I was really eager to do that, but also very concerned about the possibility that it wouldn't fly, or it wouldn't be well received. Because spin-offs, typically speaking, aren't usually successful, and Angel has proven otherwise. I mean it's really, really overcome a lot. Leaving a show like Buffy, and still maintaining that audience and bringing on new audience members and changing the dynamic even of the demographic... the fans that watch Buffy tend to be younger and female, and on Angel the demographic is more widespread – we're number one in the men's 25-36. So in some aspects it's done better, so that's really surprising.

YOU'VE NOW DONE THREE YEARS ON BOTH SERIES. HOW DO THEY COMPARE AS EXPERIENCES?

Angel feels better because I'm wiser and older and more capable of handling the change and the responsibility that comes with only three people being on the show, whereas on Buffy there was five. And I was not very high up on the totem pole as far as responsibility and screentime, and my dialog wasn't as heavy. So there were a lot more responsibilities on Angel that I had to grow into and it's worked out fine.

THERE'S AN IMPRESSION THAT ANGEL IS QUITE FUN SET TO WORK ON. WHAT DO YOU DO BETWEEN TAKES?

Everybody wants to know that. I don't know – we just hang, we talk to each other, or I'm studying my dialog with my coach, or eating, or on the phone. We hang. We engage with one another.

A KEY EPISODE, "WAITING IN THE WINGS," WAS CENTERED AROUND BALLET. YOU TRAINED AS A BALLET DANCER, SO WERE YOU SORRY YOU DIDN'T GET TO SHOW YOUR STUFF?

No. I did not want to be in tights and a leotard and a tutu.

AND HOW DID YOU FIND THE PASSIONATE SCENES WITH DAVID? WERE THEY AT ALL AWKWARD OR DIFFICULT?

Yeah, I was nervous, but I got over it.

ON A MORE MUNDANE ISSUE, YOUR HAIR WAS ORIGINALLY LONG, THEN SHORT, THEN LONG — WHAT WAS BEHIND THE LATEST STYLE?

I think I read something that David Greenwalt said, and he said it was an inside joke between the characters, and I think what he meant was that Angel prefers blondes. I'll just leave it at that.

ANOTHER BIG EPISODE LAST SEASON WAS "BIRTHDAY," WHERE CORDELIA GOT HER WISH TO BECOME A FAMOUS ACTRESS.

That was such a great episode. It's one of my favorite episodes. It was good fun to be on a sitcom because that's my secret wish.

"I'M CURIOUS TO FIND OUT WHAT'S NEXT FOR CORDELIA AS FAR AS, WHEN SHE HAS HER POWERS, WHERE ARE THEY GOING TO GO WITH THAT NOW?"

The next step for me… I would really enjoy being on a sitcom, rather than doing one-hour drama, especially on a night-time show, because the hours are completely different from a daytime drama. Obviously when you're working on a vampire show you're outside at night, and we have to go to these weird areas and it's challenging. So it would be nice to do a half hour show in a studio, because when I did that episode

"Birthday" we got to shoot the episode partly as a sitcom because I was a sitcom star, and we were out by 3pm. I mean, who knew?!? And I was trying to be quick, because I had a lot of wardrobe changes to shoot for the opening of the sitcom, and the crewmembers were like, "Oh, my wife is going to be so grateful, Charisma. Thank you so much for getting us out of here." Well, I didn't get them out of there – it was the way it was scheduled. These people don't see their families, and tend to live an hour away from Paramount Studios where we shoot, so I don't see my family, and if I have children and I get married that's going to be a grave concern for me, so I want to be on a sitcom.

AS PART OF THIS WE'VE SEEN CORDELIA GO THROUGH SOME NIGHTMARES IN HER BID TO BECOME AN ACTRESS. CAN YOU IDENTIFY WITH WHAT SHE'S BEEN THROUGH?

No. It's dramatized. Creative licensing.

IN OTHER WORK, YOU STARRED IN AN EPISODE OF STRANGE FREQUENCY PLAYING A GOTHIC ROCK STAR. WAS THAT GOOD FUN, A NICE BREAK?

Great fun. A nice break, exactly.

HOW DID THAT COME ABOUT?

It was offered by Dan Merchant who, I don't know if he followed the show, or what, but I was in Africa and I happened to be shooting Groomsmen, and I got word in Africa that they wanted me to go to Canada, so I was thrilled to do it. I knew the background, I knew that it was a music show, I loved the opportunity of being a rock star, and fake singing and stuff. I mean, I understand people's dreams to want to be a rock star fully now.

DO YOU HAVE ANY ASPIRATIONS THAT WAY?

Yeah, but you don't want me to sing 'cause it's really bad! Not even in the shower.

YOU MENTIONED THE GROOMSMEN AS WELL. HOW WAS THAT AS AN EXPERIENCE, WORKING ON A FILM LIKE THAT?

You know it wasn't really that typical because I didn't audition for the part and I didn't

have to go through any of that. I wasn't brought over by the production, I was actually visiting somebody that was working on the movie. And while I was there they were having difficulty casting the part of Kim, and so I kind of volunteered, jokingly, sort of, and then they got back to me a day later, they were really having trouble, and said, "Well, would you do it?" And I said, "You know, I don't know, call my agent, let's talk about it." So it worked out.

AND IS THIS SOMETHING YOU'D LIKE TO DO MORE OF?
Yeah.

BUFFY MIGHT END AT THE END OF THIS SEASON. IF ANGEL KEEPS ON GOING YOU WILL BE THE LONGEST SERVING PRINCIPAL CASTMEMBER FROM THE BUFFY FRANCHISE…
Maybe.

DOES IT EVER BECOME A GRIND, OR DO YOU STILL ENJOY IT?
"Does it ever become a grind?" You know what, if it wasn't for the three months between, it probably would, because it does become a long stretch. You shoot six months, that's the front, then you have a two-week vacation, and then you do the last three months. We shoot nine months out of the year. It would be ideal, especially for the crew. Like I said, I do work long hours, it is very hard, but the crewmembers are the ones who really work hard. They don't have a trailer to retreat to, they don't really have time. It's hard, and they live an hour away from where we work. And they're there every day. Sometimes I don't have to work every day. Sometimes I just have to come in for a wardrobe fitting. So that would be ideal. Sometimes it feels like a grind when I'm not in a good mood, or I'm not feeling good about… whatever. You have your moments, like everyone. But no, it's been a wonderful experience, and it's a well-oiled machine. Everybody knows what they're doing. Everybody knows where they're supposed to be

standing. Everybody comes prepared. So of course that makes things easier.

ANTHONY STEWART HEAD HAS A GOOD ARRANGEMENT WITH BUFFY AT THE MOMENT, WHERE HE HAS ORGANIZED TIME TO COME AND GO. IS THAT A CHANCE YOU'D LIKE?
I've talked about it, just in the sense that I want to be a mother. And being a mother on a show working those hours is a direct conflict. It's just not easy and I don't want to be an absentee mother. I don't want nannies. I don't want that, ideally.

SO WHERE DO YOU SEE YOURSELF HEADING IN THE FUTURE? DO YOU HAVE PLANS?
I just want to develop my personal life as well as my career.

THIS WAS THE FIRST SEASON THAT ANGEL HAS BEEN ON ITS OWN ON THE WB. HOW DO YOU FEEL IT'S DONE WITHOUT BUFFY?
Oh, great! Like I said before, the demographic has increased and we've developed new demographics, and from my limited knowledge, what I hear, we're very, very successful and I'm grateful because most spin-offs don't do well, and it's worked out quite nicely.

CHARISMA CARPENTER, THANK YOU VERY MUCH. +

KISS CHASE

CORDELIA'S LOVELIFE HAS CERTAINLY HAD ITS UPS AND DOWNS. WE CHECK OUT SOME OF HER PAST LOVES, TO FIND OUT WHO HER MR RIGHT IS...

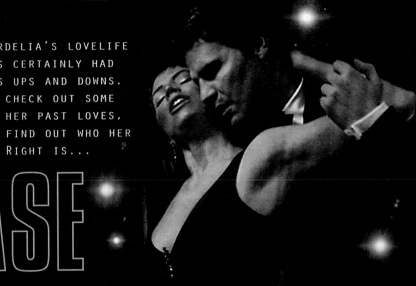

Wesley Wyndham-Pryce

WHEN: *Buffy* Season Three (final episodes)
WHAT HAPPENED: Even though he was slightly older, the two shared an attraction immediately. Unfortunately, they didn't share a very good first kiss, and it was all over pretty quickly.
TRUE LOVE? Nope. There have been no flirtations since.

Xander Harris

WHEN: *Buffy* Seasons Two and Three
WHAT HAPPENED: Cordy never would have dreamed she'd fall for Xander, but the two went out for quite a while. She dumped him to maintain her high school popularity, but she was really still in love with him, and they quickly reconciled – and then she caught him kissing Willow...
TRUE LOVE? Perhaps. Xander played a major part in Cordy's personal development, and his gesture towards her in "The Prom" (buying her a dress she couldn't afford) was extremely romantic.

Doyle

WHEN: *Angel* Season One (first half)
WHAT HAPPENED: Cordy didn't even realize the extent of her feelings for Doyle until it was too late...
TRUE LOVE? Who knows what might have happened?

Phantom Dennis

WHEN: *Angel* Season One onwards
WHAT HAPPENED: Cordy's ghostly room-mate has always done his best to look out for her – but is his protectiveness a sign of deeper feelings?
TRUE LOVE? Very one-sided.

The Haxil Beast

WHEN: "Expecting", *Angel* Season One
WHAT HAPPENED: The Haxil Beast gets one of his emissaries to impregnate Cordy with his demon spawn!
TRUE LOVE? Unsurprisingly, no. (And Angel and Wes killed him, anyway, so the romance is off!)

The Groosalugg

WHEN: *Angel* Seasons Two and Three
WHAT HAPPENED: From the time she first met Groo, Cordy was head over heels in love with him – but, unfortunately for Groo, she also started to become head over heels in love with Angel.
TRUE LOVE? Yes. Almost.

Connor

WHEN: *Angel* Season Four
WHAT HAPPENED: An end of the world romp. Hey, in that situation, who wouldn't?
TRUE LOVE? No! (?)

Angel

WHEN: *Angel* Season Three onwards (sort of).
WHAT HAPPENED: After years of knowing each other, the nature of their relationship takes a decidedly romantic turn... Until Cordy sleeps with his son!!
TRUE LOVE? Quite possibly... but the course of true love never does run smooth, does it...?

AND MR RIGHT IS...

Well, we'd say Angel, but there's that whole moment of happiness/turning evil thing... Doyle would have been good, but he's, er, dead, and Groo would have been good too, but she's burned her bridges there. So maybe Cordy should pop back to Sunnydale and hook up with Xander again. But then, there's that whole Anya thing... Well, kinda.
Ah, love, eh? So complicated! ✛

To say Cordelia's time in Los Angeles has been eventful is probably the understatement of the year — what with all the demonic pregnancies, Higher Plane shenanigans, and strange romances. Here we take a look at Cordy's *Angel* activities.

A long the way from reigning rich bitch of high school, to mother of a demon goddess, Cordelia has had more job descriptions in her supernatural résumé than anyone in the *Buffy/Angel* universe. She arrives in Los Angeles fresh from high school, intending to take Hollywood by storm and become the next big star. Instead, she becomes one of thousands of unemployed actresses living in a trashy apartment and scrounging for her place in the sun. After Angel saves her from a nasty vampire, she realizes that staying out of the sun might be a good thing, and hires herself as Angel's office manager.

Maybe working for a vampire and a half-demon isn't the greatest item for a would-be actor's résumé, but at least it's going to be a steady paycheck, if Cordelia has anything to say about it. She insists that her broody boss start billing people for saving their lives. Not that it's easy collecting on invoices with entries like "remove extra demon eye from child's head," but the money side seems to work out okay. Before long, Cordy is able to afford a much better apartment — once ghost-mom-from-hell is exorcised — and she certainly isn't making that kind of money doing commercials! For most of her life,

having enough money has been the focus of Cordy's existence – that and having a steady boyfriend. Shallow? Definitely! But not too surprising in a woman who grew up with all the money she could want, until the IRS caught up with her parents. However, now that Cordy is working for a genuine Champion of Good, shallowness may not be permitted. It seems as if the Powers That Be have plans to make her a genuine good guy.

POWER GIRL

The Powers' first little gifts to Cordelia are Doyle's visions. The minute the first vision socks her between the eyes, money becomes the least of her worries. First, the visions themselves are excruciatingly painful – and quite embarrassing in the middle of an audition. It's bad enough to be left limp and moaning with a headache worse than a migraine. What Cordelia sees in the visions would make even a valley girl older and wiser, what with murder, torture, terror, and mayhem unfolding right inside her head where she can't look away. On top of that, the visions make Cordy a target for half the nasty creatures in L.A., beginning with the headhunters who try to auction her psychic eyeballs and ending with Wolfram & Hart, who first try to buy her eyeballs (without her attached), then attack her

THE LIFE AND TIMES OF
CORDELIA C

BY K. STO

HASE

> "I WAS THE DITZIEST BITCH IN SUNNYDALE, COULDA HAD ANY MAN I WANTED. NOW I'M ALL SUPERHERO-Y AND THE BEST ACTION I CAN GET IS AN INVISIBLE GHOST WHO'S GOOD WITH A LOOFAH." ("WAITING IN THE WINGS")

and Angel through the visions on two different occasions.

But the visions also give Cordelia something she's never had before – an important role in the fight against evil. She's not just a manager or a socialite, she's a real player, a sort of champion herself. By the time she's been vision queen for two years, Cordy knows those visions are as important to her as they are to Angel. When she learns that Groosalugg is supposed to take them from her when they mate, she refuses, because the visions have become an essential part of who she is. The next step she takes along the vision path is even more ironic. Since the visions are life-threatening to your average human, Cordy agrees to become part-demon, just so she can survive having them. Who'd have foreseen that when she was the reigning queen of normal at Sunnydale High?

And who'd have foreseen that the aspiring actress would someday care more about being a champion of good, than about becoming a star? When Angel goes to the dark side over Darla, and fires his friends, Cordelia doesn't cut her losses and return to her acting career. She sticks with Gunn and Wesley, carrying on the good fight that Angel seems to have abandoned. Of course, she's still Cordelia, the queen of petty, and she makes a big deal of refusing to even speak his name. When Angel finally comes to his senses and asks to join the team again, it's especially tough for Cordelia to forgive him. She's not so much angry that he went off the deep end obsessing with Darla, which is completely understandable, given their history. But turning his back on his friends in his darkest hour, and

actually firing them – that hurt her feelings, big time. It takes time for her to get over the hurt – exactly as much time as Angel needs to go on a major shopping spree and bring her the goodies. For all her vision wisdom, Cordy's still a material girl, and clothes and accessories are one way to her heart – or at least, her forgiveness.

TRUE ROMANCE?

What's better than being vision queen? Being a real queen, of course, and the visions lead directly to that big promotion. When Cordy first falls into Pylea, she's made a slave, shoveling demon horse poo. Not exactly the kind of job she was raised for. But once the Pyleans discover her visions, she's instantly elevated to the status of ruler – and doesn't she love it! The clothes (or near lack of them in her scanty princess costume), the jewels, the instant obeying of all her orders, and especially the handsome and adoring warrior, the Groosalugg, who is destined to be her consort. Still, the high school

Cordelia would have basked in all those princess perks without thinking of anyone else. Now, though, Cordelia's first concern, once she's sure she'll survive, is to save her friends; and her second concern is to save Pylea from the priests' oppression. Once that's taken care of, she leaves Groosalugg to carry out the social reforms, and gives up the princess gig to return to L.A. with her friends.

Considering Cordelia's views on the indispensability of having a man, her

Cordy's GUYS

Russell Winters

Only a girl from the Hellmouth's hometown could make a date with a vampire. Cordy's big evening with him leads her to Angel Investigations, and Winters to a short, hot flight. ("City of")

Phantom Dennis

It's puppy love for Dennis, who washes Cordy's back, adjusts the lights and music, and tries to protect her from nasty visitors. ("Rm w/a Vu")

willingness to leave her would-be Prince Charming shows the other big way she has changed. The one thing that's not on Cordelia's résumé is happy romance – with anyone. Sure, Angel develops strong feelings for her and she for him. And becoming part-demon would make her a better match for a vampire with a soul. But then there's Angel's broody, taciturn stuff, and all the people that keep getting in the way, like Darla and Groo, and the occasional apocalypse.

Fred is the first to see the potential of these feelings, when she sees Angel training Cordelia to fight, and tells him about 'kyerumption' – a Pylean word that means two heroes recognizing they're meant for each other. That opens Angel's eyes, but when he tries to talk to Cordy about his feelings, he's so broody and tongue-tied that she completely clues out, and thinks he's just expressing family affection for the whole gang. Before she can clue in, Darla shows up, very pregnant – and that really messes up the budding romance. Cordy's furious that Angel lied to her about sleeping with Darla, and especially that he knocked her up. Cordy is so busy verbally punishing him that she takes Darla's side, forgetting that Darla is not just a wronged woman but a very dangerous vampire. It's a near fatal mistake – but one that gives Angel a chance to show how much he cares about Cordy: he threatens to kill Darla, child or no child, if she touches Cordy again. Ain't love grand?

Wesley

Cordelia went for Wes' British class in Sunnydale, and she starts their relationship in L.A. with a big smooch – but only to get rid of Doyle's visions.

Doyle

The attraction is mutual, but Doyle is too shy to ask Cordy out, until it's too late. We'll never know if she could have loved a guy with a demon face like a hedgehog.

Despite the surface attraction, no genuine sparks ever jump between these two.

Wilson Christopher

Rich, handsome and horny, Wilson seems like Cordy's dream date – until he impregnates her with a demon's spawn. ("Expecting")

The Groosalugg

Cordy's personal knight in shining armor would do anything for his princess, including all the Com-shuking any girl could want.

Angel

Two people unlucky in love trying to have a romance is Mission: Impossible. First Darla gets in the way, then Groo. Then a trip to the ballet stokes the flames – but Angel is too broody and taciturn to express his feelings until it's too late. Why are heroes always so tongue-tied?

Connor

It's easy to understand what Connor, all adolescent hormones, sees in Cordy – including a chance to take something away from Dad. But only a few months earlier, Cordy was practically Connor's mom! Does anyone else feel queasy? Or is that just morning sickness?

SUNS AND LOVERS

The birth of Connor seems like a good chance for Cordy to discover more about her feelings for Angel, especially as the two get to do a lot of father-surrogate mother bonding over the baby. If that weren't enough to warm the fires, they also get to re-enact the passionate love story of a cursed ballerina. Given the amount of undressing and heavy breathing involved, you'd expect that experience to be the perfect way for Cordy and Angel to finally get past their bashfulness. Instead, both of them can't get out of that room fast enough to get away from all those hot and heavy feelings. Is Cordy mixed up about all this? You bet. One minute she's miffed that Angel wants to ignore their mutual feelings and put the whole thing behind them; the next minute Groo walks in, and she throws herself into his arms.

By the time Cordy realizes that Groo isn't what she wants after all, the whole Holtz and Connor apocalypse has started again. Cordelia uses her remarkable demon powers to save the day a couple of times – especially when she cleans all the hell dimension mojo out of Connor, just by turning up the lights. But she and Angel never have a chance to get together, because she's on her way to meet him, when Skip catches up with her and ushers her to a higher plain of existence.

It's still up for debate whether Cordelia deserved to become a Higher Being on her own merit, or whether that whole transcendence thing was all part of Jasmine's plan to come into this world. What Cordelia was when she came back to Earth now seems fairly clear. Threatened with eternal agony, Skip tells Angel that the real Cordelia is "in there somewhere, she's just not driving." Jasmine's spirit is in control, using not only Cordy's body, but her personality.

The Cordelia who came back from the Higher Plain looks, talks and acts like Cordy, but it's Cordy at her worst: manipulative, self-centered, ready to do anything to get her own way. When she tells Angel she can't be with him, because of all the things he did as Angelus, she sounds really noble and sincere – until you compare her to the woman who helped him get over losing baby Connor, and took away Connor's evil. Then the new Cordy sounds incredibly lame. And when she sleeps with Connor, not even her speeches about the end of the world and giving Connor something real, can hide how seriously she's messed up. The Cordelia who changed Connor's nappies couldn't possibly sleep with him. We find out just know how messed up she is, when she frees Angelus, murders Lilah, and finally runs off with Connor. It's Angel who says, with absolute conviction, "This thing isn't Cordelia."

With Jasmine's birth, even the sham Cordelia is gone, her will drawn into Jasmine, her body left in a coma. But the Powers That Be still owe Cordy one last favor, and Cordy uses it to come back from her coma, and help the man she loves get back on track one last time, when he seems to have given up all hope. With a final kiss, Cordy passes on her visions to Angel, and bids him a tearful farewell, knowing that her job is finally done. When the hospital rings Angel to inform him of Cordy's death, it's a heartbreaking loss – a lover, a friend, and a true champion, gone – but certainly never forgotten. ✛

{
WILLOW: "HOW'VE YOU BEEN?"
CORDELIA: "HIGHER POWER. YOU?"
WILLOW: "ULTIMATE EVIL, BUT
I GOT BETTER."("ORPHEUS")
}

SEASON FIVE EPISODE 12

"YOU'RE WELCOME"

Original U.S. airdate: February 4, 2004 • Original U.K. airdate: March 30, 2004

Synopsis

Sick and tired of defending evil, Angel's about ready to throw in the towel. As if on queue, Cordelia Chase suddenly awakens from her coma and is shocked to discover that Angel and the gang are now running things at the evil law firm, Wolfram & Hart. With Angel off track, having lost all his conviction, it's up to Cordy to give him a kick up the ass and get him back into the game. Meanwhile, Lindsey McDonald sets about trying to bring Angel down, once and for all.

With seemingly super-human strength, he gets to kick Angel's ass – briefly. After defeating Lindsey, Angel and Cordy share a tender moment in Angel's office. But a phone call interrupts their reunion. It's the hospital, informing Angel of Cordelia's death. It seems she never actually awoke from her coma.

Memorable Dialogue

Cordelia: "I'm a vision of hotliness… Mystical comas. You know, if you can stand the horror of a higher power hijacking your mind and body so that it can give birth to itself, I really recommend 'em."

Cordelia: "Spike's a hero, and you're C.E.O. of Hell, Incorporated. What freakin' bizarro world did I wake up in?"

Cordelia: "Don't make this hard, Angel. I'm just on a different road… and this is my off-ramp. The Powers That Be owed me one, and I didn't waste it. I got my guy back on track."

Guest Star Info: Christian Kane

Born on June 27, in Dallas, Texas, Christian spent most of his formative years in Norman, Oklahoma. He attended the University of Oklahoma, where he had plans to major in Art History. However, Christian wanted to try his hand at acting, so he dropped out. After gathering together his life savings, Christian got in his truck and headed to Hollywood. In 1997 he was signed up to star in a new TV show called *Fame L.A.* Based on the hit movie and popular 80s TV series, it gave Christian the perfect opportunity to showcase his singing and acting talents. But, after just 22 episodes, the show got canceled. His next role came along in the shape of Aaron Spelling's *Rescue 77*, a drama about L.A. fire fighters. But, once again, poor ratings led to the show's demise. Then along came *Angel*…

Statistics

 No. of times Angel kicks ass: 3

 No. of smooches: 2

 No. of deaths: 7 (5 nuns, 1 demon, 1 human)

 No. of times Angel and Spike trade blows: 1

Trivia

- This is *Angel*'s 100th episode.

- Joss Whedon was responsible for writing the final scene between Angel and Cordelia. Apparently, both David and Charisma were really crying during several takes. Aww, bless.

 Episode Credits

Written by:	David Fury
Directed by:	David Fury
Angel:	David Boreanaz
Cordelia Chase:	Charisma Carpenter
Spike:	James Marsters
Wesley Wyndam-Pryce:	Alexis Denisof

Charles Gunn:	J. August Richards
Winifred Burkle:	Amy Acker
Lorne:	Andy Hallett
Harmony:	Mercedes McNab
Doyle:	Glenn Quinn
Lindsey:	Christian Kane

IRISH EYES

By Mike Stokes

THE ROAD RISES UP TO MEET GLENN
QUINN AS HE RETURNS TO TELEVISION
AS *ANGEL*'S GUARDIAN ANGEL

G lenn Quinn didn't set out to be an actor when he moved with his mother and sisters to the United States from Dublin, Ireland, eleven years ago. He was actually spotted by casting director Johanna Ray (*Twin Peaks, Blue Velvet, Wild at Heart*) who saw something special in him. She helped Quinn find an agent and before long, he was auditioning for a guest spot on *Roseanne* in 1990, which he spun into an eight season run.

Talking to Quinn, it's not hard to see why success found him early. He's got the piercing eyes and rugged good looks of a leading man, with the devilish grin of the neighborhood pal who used to get you in trouble by making you laugh in church. Factor in a little luck o' the Irish and a repertoire of dead-on impersonations ranging from *Sesame Street*'s loveable Grover to intense character actor Christopher Walken, and you've got the makings of a natural showman.

GLENN QUINN *Doyle*

He is best known for his role as the convincingly-American-accented Mark Healy, Becky Conner's (played by both Lecy Goranson and Sarah Chalke throughout the years) ne'er do well boyfriend and eventual husband on *Roseanne*. His list of credits also includes an on-screen kiss with Oscar winner Gwynneth Paltrow in 1991's *Shout*, the short-lived but critically acclaimed television series *Covington Cross*, and horror fare including 1997's *Campfire Tales* and 1992's *Dr. Giggles*.

Now with a starring role in *Angel*, Quinn journeys to the darker side of acting once again as the good-hearted demon Doyle. The role seems tailor-made for Quinn; Doyle's a fun-loving Irishman with a serious side when it comes to the business at hand—usually saving lives and acting as a streetwise guardian angel to his brooding vampire friend.

He and Angel himself, David Boreanaz, have also become friends. Quinn hung out a bit with Boreanaz and his wife (who shares the same last name as Quinn, but is no relation) during a vacation over the summer in Ireland.

While Quinn is immersed in the Hollywood spotlight and Doyle attempts to remain one of Los Angeles' underground secrets, both are down-to-earth characters using their gifts for good. Both the character Doyle and the actor Quinn seem like the kind of guys you'd like to sit down with and share a couple pints of Guinness while they tell stories of supernatural acquaintances or what it's like to work with John Travolta. While Goldfingers, the L.A. nightclub Quinn co-owns with friend and fellow Irishman Mark Leddy, isn't nearly big enough to seat the millions of fans who will be tuning-in to see the October 5th debut of *Angel*, we humbly offer this interview instead. Read and enjoy with the beverage of your choice. Cheers!

takes us." Sometimes I tried to do that when I went in to read for things, so the Irish thing just really clicked.

BTM: MANY PEOPLE ARE PROBABLY WONDERING IF YOU'LL BE CONVINCING AS IRISHMAN DOYLE. SINCE YOU WERE BORN AND RAISED IN IRELAND AND NATURALLY SPEAK WITH AN IRISH BROGUE IN REAL LIFE, HOW DO YOU LIKE YOUR CHANCES?
GLENN QUINN: What do you think? [laughs] I was just back in Ireland, and the accent's not real thick, but it's definitely audible. It should be an interesting and memorable character. It'll definitely appeal to a lot of people.

BTM: WAS IT TOUGH TO PICK UP THE AMERICAN ACCENT?
GQ: Not at all. I've done a couple of T.V. movies, and I had done a film with John Travolta [1991's *Shout*], and all of a sudden I went in on a guest-starring role for *Roseanne*, much like David [Boreanaz] did on *Buffy*, and they kept me on. It was really successful. I have no problems doing the accent, because I've always been mimicking people my whole life.

BTM: WHAT WAS IT LIKE WALKING INTO A TOP RATED SHOW AND SUDDENLY BEING FAMOUS?
GQ: At that time, *Roseanne* was number one, and I don't even think I knew what I was getting into. It was so huge, it was amazing to get on that show.

BTM: HOW DOES DOING AN HOUR-LONG SERIES COMPARE TO WORKING ON A SITCOM?
GQ: Well, you've got to figure what we do in one and a half days on *Angel* was my whole week on *Roseanne*. This is like mak-

GLENN QUINN

I HAVE NO PROBLEMS DOING THE ACCENT, BECAUSE I'VE ALWAYS BEEN MIMICKING PEOPLE MY WHOLE LIFE.

BUFFY THE MAGAZINE: U2 OR IRON MAIDEN?
GLENN QUINN: U2, of course. The boys! They're my boys. They're good guys.

BTM: DID YOU KNOW DOYLE WAS IRISH BEFORE YOU AUDITIONED?
GQ: It was an interesting thing. I went and I read it American and [Joss Whedon] said, "Hey, let's do this Irish and see where it

ing a nine month movie. It's definitely a lot harder. You say goodbye to your normal life as you know it. It's a challenge, it keeps you out of trouble, and it keeps you on the go.

BTM: DID YOU KNOW MUCH ABOUT *BUFFY THE VAMPIRE SLAYER* WHEN YOU WERE CALLED ABOUT DOING *ANGEL*?
GQ: Not anything.

Whistler's OTHER

Astute fans of *Buffy the Vampire Slayer* will remember Whistler as the mysterious stranger lending a helping hand to to a pathetic, rat-eating Angel back in Manhattan of 1996. He helped the vampire get acclimated to the world he'd tried to avoid for 90 years, surprising Angel with the knowledge that he not only knew he was a vampire, but also that he'd been given back his human soul. It turns out Whistler is one of many demons that is not dedicated to the destruction of all life. He's an immortal who's been sent to even the score between good and evil—or at least keep the spread pretty close. With the introduction of Doyle, another demon who knows all about Angel before the two even meet, it'll be impossible not to draw comparisons between Angel's two compadres. But rest assured, while the characters have some traits in common, each has his own very distinct personality. The chart below should help sort out what Whistler and Doyle have in common as well as where they differ:

VS

	DOYLE	WHISTLER
Actor	Glenn Quinn	Max Perlich
Debut	*Angel* episode #1-1 "City of Angel"	*Buffy* episode #2-21 "Becoming, Part 1"
Descent	Ireland	United States (probably Cleveland)
Quirk	He's a Demon	He's a Demon
Hobbies	Drinking, gambling, trying to woo women	Drinking
Power	Visions	Seems to know things, probably also has visions
Curse	Visions cause splitting headaches	Nobody understands him, which can be a headache
Home Base	Los Angeles	New York
Style	Black leather coats, big collars	Black leather coats, big collars, hat
Buffy Link	Tries to help Angel get over her	Introduces Angel to her
Found Angel	Brooding in private	Brooding in the gutter

BTM: IN ANGEL'S PAST THERE WAS ANOTHER DEMON NAMED WHISTLER THAT HELPED HIM OUT. IS DOYLE AN UPDATE ON THAT CHARACTER OR IS THE SAME TYPE OF ROLE?

GQ: They actually sent me those tapes, and it turns out that the guy who played Whistler, Max Perlich, is a friend. I don't know if there's a little bit of Whistler in Doyle, but I don't think he is Whistler at all.

BTM: DOYLE HAS THESE VISIONS FROM TIME TO TIME. HAVE YOU EVER HAD ANY PSYCHIC EXPERIENCES?

GQ: No, but quite a number of women have told me that I am psychic. [Nonchalantly] Mmm-hmm. I know where the buttons are [laughs]. Or where they're not, depending on who you're talking to.

BTM: HAVE YOU FORESEEN BECOMING A BIG-TIME T.V. HERO AND A POPULAR TEEN HEARTTHROB?

GQ: Everybody's saying that to me. I've kind of gone through that, but I never did any publicity on *Roseanne*. Everybody used to go, "We like that guy, but why isn't he doing anything?" This is more of a featured role. It's a great showcase for me, and whatever comes is really part of the whole package. You've got to do that and keep a level head on you.

BTM: HAVE YOU HAD ANY PREVIOUS EXPERIENCE WITH VAMPIRES?

GQ: No, but I come alive at night. I'm definitely a night person, and I've been into the whole vampire thing for years. Ever since I was a kid, I've always imagined being one. I hate the sun.

BTM: SO YOU PROBABLY DON'T MIND THE MANY ANGEL NIGHT SHOOTS?

GQ: Actually, it really screws you up. You don't know what day it is. The weeks are flying by here. This is Thursday already, but I feel like it's still Monday, yet the weekend is right around the corner. It's very odd.

BTM: DO YOU EVER GET STUCK WITH A LATE NIGHT SHOOT FOLLOWED-UP BY AN EARLY MORNING CALL?

GQ: They have to give you a 12-hour turnaround— that's the union law.

BTM: MUCH LIKE YOURSELF, DOYLE SEEMS TO LIKE THE NIGHTLIFE, HE HAS AN EYE FOR THE LADIES AND WORKS ODD HOURS WITH DAVID BOREANAZ. WHERE DOES GLENN QUINN STOP AND THE DOYLE CHARACTER BEGIN?

GQ: Glenn and Doyle are all one. I take over where he leaves off. I suppose it's a vicious circle.

BTM: EXCEPT FOR THE PART ABOUT DOYLE BEING A DEMON?

GQ: I've always been a devil.

GLENN QUINN *Doyle*

DOYLE DOESN'T WANT ANY
THE FIGHTING. ALTHOUGH
WANT ANYTHING TO DO

BTM: What was your impression of the character when you first learned about who and what he is?

GQ: I had a lot to bring to him, and when they gave me a character description, I was all over it. Every day, you get another little pinch of what he's all about. Everyday, you try another shoe on, and it fits. It's really groovy, man. It's a lot of fun to screw around with.

BTM: Of all Doyle's quirks and personality traits, what's your favorite?

GQ: His sense of humor, I think. He doesn't want anything to do with all the fighting and all that. Although he has to, he doesn't want anything to do with it. He'd rather be on a plane to Vegas.

BTM: For a pacifist, your character is in a pretty dangerous line of work and in a pretty seedy part of Los Angeles. What was the worst job you've ever had?

> **THING TO DO WITH ALL HE HAS TO, HE DOESN'T WITH IT.**

GQ: Which one? There were so many of them. I was working on power plants when I first came here and that really sucked. A lot of insulation removal and all that crap. It was a pain in the ass.

BTM: Angel and Doyle may be friends, but they have very different personalities. For example, Angel tends to brood a lot, whereas Doyle likes to party. Eventually even the best of friends get on each other's nerves, so if the two characters clash, who wins the fight?

GQ: I think that, of course, him being around longer, he might. But who knows who has the upper hand? We're gonna have to wait, I suppose, until it lands on paper, but I think [the producers] are talking about it. We don't know what Doyle's all about yet. Slowly but surely, they're revealing more and more to me and to everybody else. Hypothetically, he'd probably beat the crap out of me, and I'd just drink the pain away.

BTM: All right, not to start trouble, but let's say Boreanaz ticks you off and the two of you throw down. Who going to win that celebrity deathmatch?

GQ: Oh, easy. I'd take him. [laughs] I think it'd be an even fight and we'd sit around after and laugh about it.

BTM: It seems like you, David Boreanaz and Charisma Carpenter get along well and are having a really good time together. Is that accurate?

GQ: Everybody's got their feet firmly on the ground. There's only three of us now, you've got to remember that, whereas, *Buffy* was a bigger ensemble, but there's no egos flying around here. David's great, Charisma's a doll, and I didn't bring any crap from the other show over. I'm just grateful to be working, because there's a lot of people that aren't.

BTM: How about the guys running the show? Being the new guy, what's been your impression of David Greenwalt and Joss Whedon?

GQ: David's a real terrific guy. You got to figure, they created these characters from the success of *Buffy*. I mean, they're very smart, intelligent people. They're doing it for a reason.

BTM: Did you already know Joss Whedon from your previous work when you auditioned for the part of Doyle?

GQ: I didn't, no, but I heard that he used to write on *Roseanne* the first season. But I didn't know him.

BTM: Would you describe Doyle more as a Robin to Angel's Batman or are the two of them more like Wonder Twins?

GQ: He's not really a sidekick. He's more of a mentor and kind of lectures Angel on what to do and what not to do, but won't really get involved himself, because he'd much rather be out having a drink or playing the track or in Vegas having fun. But he's definitely a pal.

BTM: So you're not concerned with changing the show's name to *Doyle*?

GQ: David's a good actor. It's his name leading the show in, and I didn't mind play-

ing second to him at all. He's a great guy and a good actor, and the two of us together, I think, are really good. And it's not cheesey, because I didn't want to do anything cheesey, obviously—who would? I think it's going to turn out really well.

BTM: One of your past projects, *Campfire Tales*, which had some scenes directed by frequent *Buffy* director David Semel, has been making the rounds on cable lately.

GQ: That was the worst thing I've ever done. I did that in a two week gap of *Roseanne*, and I looked really bad. David Semel's a great guy—I hear he's going to come in and do an episode of *Angel*. It would be fun to work with him again.

BTM: We liked *Campfire Tales* and were kind of hoping for news of a sequel. Bummer. ✛

By
K. Stoddard Hayes

HIS TIME IN THE *ANGEL*VERSE MAY HAVE BEEN SHORT, BUT THE IMPACT HE HAD ON ANGEL'S JOURNEY TO REDEMPTION WAS HUGE. GONE, BUT NOT FORGOTTEN BY EITHER TEAM ANGEL OF VIEWERS ALIKE, WE TAKE A LOOK BACK AT THE LIFE AND TIMES OF THAT LOVEABLE HALF-DEMON, ALLEN FRANCIS DOYLE...

He's a man of many talents. He knows where to get the history of a building on the internet, or the obscure ingredients for a rare spell in the Los Angeles underground. He knows a guy who can get a beautiful rent-controlled apartment for a friend (as long as the friend doesn't mind a little ghostly company). He's culturally savvy, being a fan of professional sports, Batman, and *Angela's Ashes*, and he can spot when a woman has a stylish new pair of shoes. He can talk faster than many a bad guy out to collect his hide, and can down a pint of beer with the best – or a glass of single-malt scotch, in a pinch. He can use his demon senses to find the hiding place of a precious magic artifact like the Gem of Amarra. And most important, he has visions that can help a champion save the helpless from the forces of evil.

So why would such a gifted guy live in a run-down apartment littered with his own trash, and devote most of his time and money to betting on sports – and hiding from the muscle demons the bookies send to collect? Meet the puzzle that is Allen Francis Doyle, the friendly, Irish, half-Brachen demon, and messenger of the Powers that Be.

When Angel asks about Doyle's loser lifestyle, Doyle explains, "It's the kind of life that keeps you from having your expectations too high" ("Rm w/a Vu"). Doyle has fallen a long way in his short life, from a normal human childhood and a happy marriage, to that run-down bachelor dive. And it's all his fault. Now he has so little trust in himself that he

won't risk further disappointment by trying to get more out of life.

Doyle's life came apart because of a pervasive bigotry against demons – and Doyle has been his own chief bigot. From the start, we get numerous hints that he doesn't like his demon half. Every time something (a sneeze or a punch) makes his face break out in bristles, he comments that he hates it! When Angel asks him why he won't fight in demon face, even though it makes him stronger, Doyle responds, rather lamely, that it's not his style. He won't tell Cordelia he's a demon, because he's afraid she'll reject him – but really, he has already rejected himself as a potential date for her. As she tells him when she finally learns the truth, half demon is way down on the list, after short and poor. It was Doyle who decided that being half demon made him

not good enough for a girl like Cordelia, just as it made him "not good enough" for his wife, Harry.

Doyle didn't learn about his demon side until he was grown and married. The revelation shocked and disgusted him, so much that he sank into self-hatred. Though Harry was fascinated and began learning about demons, Doyle persuaded himself that his wife couldn't possibly love a half-demon, that she must be just pretending. Convinced that she must be as revolted by his demon nature as he was himself, he drove her into leaving him. Years later, Harry tells Angel that she left not because of Doyle's demon nature, but because of his self-loathing ("The Bachelor Party").

Sadly, the ruin of his marriage wasn't the end of his disintegration. "Why you?" Angel asks, when Doyle explains his mission as Vision Boy. Doyle replies, with uncharacteristic terseness, "We all got something to atone for" ("City Of"). That something was a band of Brachen demons, Doyle's own race, that came to him soon after his marriage ended. The Brachens begged him to help them escape the Scourge, a blood-thirsty military movement that was dedicated to eradicating all whose demon blood was impure. But Doyle's loathing of all-things-demon almost

matched the hatred of the Scourge. He turned his back on the Brachens, and all of them were massacred ("Hero").

The visions came to Doyle just at that time in his life. Now, years later, he agrees to put them to good use, as part of his atonement for that sin. The mission he gives Angel, of "reaching out to people, showing them there's still hope" is intended by the Powers partly to help fulfill Angel's potential. It never occurs to Doyle that his association with Angel – and Cordelia – might give him hope as well, and help him as much as it's supposed to help Angel.

From the start, he's determined to stay safe in his own little world, and serve as no more than a messenger and guide. Though he'll tell Angel about each vision and encourage him to follow the Powers' program, he plans to stay well out of the action. Too bad he overlooked Angel's recent history with the Scoobies. Angel is used to everyone pitching in to fight the good fight, and he makes Doyle the driver for the mission to Russell Winters' house. "I'm not combat ready! I'm just the messenger!" Doyle protests in alarm. "I'm the message," Angel retorts, promoting Doyle from messenger to sidekick.

To his own surprise, Doyle finds he's more the hero than he wants to be.

When he hears gunfire inside Winters' mansion, he rabbits – for about 100 feet. Then, swearing at himself, he turns the Angelmobile around and drives to the rescue. From then on, he's enlisted, as research associate (since Cordelia is useless with the computer), as bodyguard, escorting clients safely home, even as muscle – of a sort. In no time at all, the guy who ran at the sound of gunfire is standing up to some of the scariest people, including no less than William the Bloody, Spike himself, when Doyle and Cordy brave his torture chamber to rescue Angel ("In the Dark"). When Cordelia is jumped by a vampire on Angel's doorstep, Doyle doesn't just run for help, he takes on the vamp and kills him. And as Cordelia points out, even though he's well beaten up, his first concern is to ask whether Cordy is okay ("The Bachelor Party").

In this instance, Doyle is not inspired only by Angel's heroic example. With Cordelia in mortal danger, he never thinks of running. Only weeks into their relationship, he's genuinely smitten, and not just with her looks. Doyle's flirtation with Cordelia may look at first like a guy coming on to a hot girl to score a

big date, but it quickly becomes much more, at least to Doyle. He's obsessed with her; many of his lightest words are full of flirtatious double-*entendres*, and he's always hatching schemes to go out with her. And unknown to him, it's working. The queen of gold-diggers, who's always measured a guy's eligibility by the size of his portfolio, finds herself thinking that maybe other qualities are more important, like the courage Doyle showed in beating off the vampire. Cordelia's acceptance of Doyle is an important moment of redemption for the half-demon. He lost his wife because he couldn't accept his demon side; now that he can accept it, he has a chance to win the love of another woman.

However, one essential piece of Doyle's past still has to be reckoned with. When the Scourge returns to Los Angeles, hunting a peaceful clan of Lister demons, Doyle has his chance to atone for his past sins, and, to his own surprise, to become a hero. When the moment comes when someone must die to disarm the Beacon, the Scourge's terrible Weapon of Mass Destruction that will kill every human or part human for

blocks, Angel steps up to sacrifice himself – and finds Doyle in his way. "You never know 'til you're tested," he says, and knocks Angel off the catwalk. He kisses Cordelia and passes on the visions, so that the mission will survive his passing. And that one brief kiss is all the happiness Doyle gets in this life. "Too bad we never get to find out whether this is a face you could love," he tells her, as he morphs into demon face for the last time and sacrifices himself to save the Lister demons from the Scourge. ✥

The Messenger's Report Card

In "Soul Purpose," Lindsey presents himself to Spike as a vision-wielding guide and mentor named "Doyle." How well does the vengeful ex-lawyer do with his Doyle impersonation?

Visions: Doyle describes his visions as migraines with pictures. Lindsey tells Spike they're like an ice cream brain-freeze. Wuss! Oh, yeah, and they're fake. *GRADE: B*

Wardrobe: Doyle's tan leather jacket and colorful shirts fit in with his sports geek/compulsive gambler lifestyle. Lindsey's "urban cowboy" duds are sleek, but very short on personality. *GRADE: B*

Apartment procurement: Doyle finds Cordelia a sunny, stylish (if slightly haunted) rent-controlled flat. Lindsey finds Spike a basement that looks like the inside of a cheap mobile home. At least it has sewer access. *GRADE: C*

Booze: Doyle celebrates every occasion with a six-pack of Colt 45, and is partial to single-malt whiskey as an antidote to visions. Lindsey invites himself into Spike's flat and helps himself to the beer. *GRADE: C*

Back-up: Doyle never intended to be more than a messenger, but before he knows it, he's driving getaway, guarding clients, beating up demons, and shooting vampires. Lindsey makes sure he remains only a messenger, staying on the sidelines and out of sight. *GRADE: F*

Friendliness: Doyle gets Angel out among the lost and lonely, and even gets on his payroll to help end his isolation. Lindsey makes sure Spike has no payroll and stays away from anyone who might befriend him. *GRADE: F*

CLASSIC SCENE

"Hero"

"You never know until you've been tested."

The Story so far...

Angel Investigations attempts to save a group of helpless half-demons from The Scourge, an army of pure-blood demons on a mission to wipe out humans and half-blood demons. Unfortunately, The Scourge has in their possession a machine capable of destroying humans. And they have Team Angel and a ship full of innocent demons (yes, innocent demons!) cornered and about to be wiped out.

The Scene...

A FREIGHT SHIP IN A HARBOR SOMEWHERE IN LOS ANGELES.

(In the cargo hold of the freighter, things look bleak for Angel and Co. as The Scourge close in on them. It gets worse when the machine capable of mass destruction kicks into life...)

DOYLE: What does that thing do?
ANGEL: Its light kills anything with human blood.
DOYLE: Well, it's getting brighter and that doohickey – it's fully armed, isn't it?
ANGEL: Almost. If I pull the cable, I think I can still shut it off.
DOYLE: How're you gonna do that without touching the light?
CORDELIA: Angel, that's suicide.
DOYLE: There's got to be another way.
ANGEL: (Looks at the demons, then at Cordelia.) It's all right.
CORDELIA: No!
DOYLE: (Puts his hand on Angel's arm.) The good fight, yeah? You never know until you've been tested. I get that now.

(Doyle suddenly hits Angel with a hard right to the chin, knocking him down. He turns to Cordy and kisses her. A strange blue light appears between their lips just before they part.)

DOYLE: Too bad we'll never know (morphs into his demon face) if this is a face you could learn to love.

(Angel picks himself up off the floor, runs over to the ladder and climbs back up.)

ANGEL: Doyle. Doyle. Doyle! Doyle! NO!

(Doyle jumps over to the beacon just before Angel reaches the platform. He grabs a hold of the metal frame, turns his head and smiles at Angel and Cordy.)

ANGEL: No!

(Doyle tries to pull the cable connection apart as the light gets brighter and starts to melt the skin off his face. Everybody watches spellbound as Doyle manages to pull the cable apart just before he burns up. The beacon goes dark. Cordy starts crying and Angel pulls her into a hug, teary-eyed himself.)

EPISODE CREDITS

Season One, Episode Nine
first aired: 11/30/99 (US) & 03/03/2000(UK)
written by: Howard Gordon
directed by: Tucker Gates
Main actors this scene:
Doyle: Glen Quinn
Angel: David Boreanaz
Cordelia: Charisma Carpenter

WHY SO COOL?

No way! We're barely into the series (well, nine episodes down) and they go and kill off one of the show's main characters!! Total shocker!! Whilst the death of a beloved character like Doyle can hardly be described as cool *per se*, offing a popular character is a good way to keep fans on their toes. And he did have the most noble of deaths.

EPISODE TRIVIA

The opening scene of this episode is actually from David Fury's original script for the show's second episode, "Corrupt." The un-produced script reads the same word-for-word as it does in this episode.

Before working on *Buffy* and *Angel*, Howard Gordon wrote 20 episodes of *The X-Files*. He is currently working as an executive producer and writer on hit show, *24*.

Compiled by Kate Anderson

Doyle

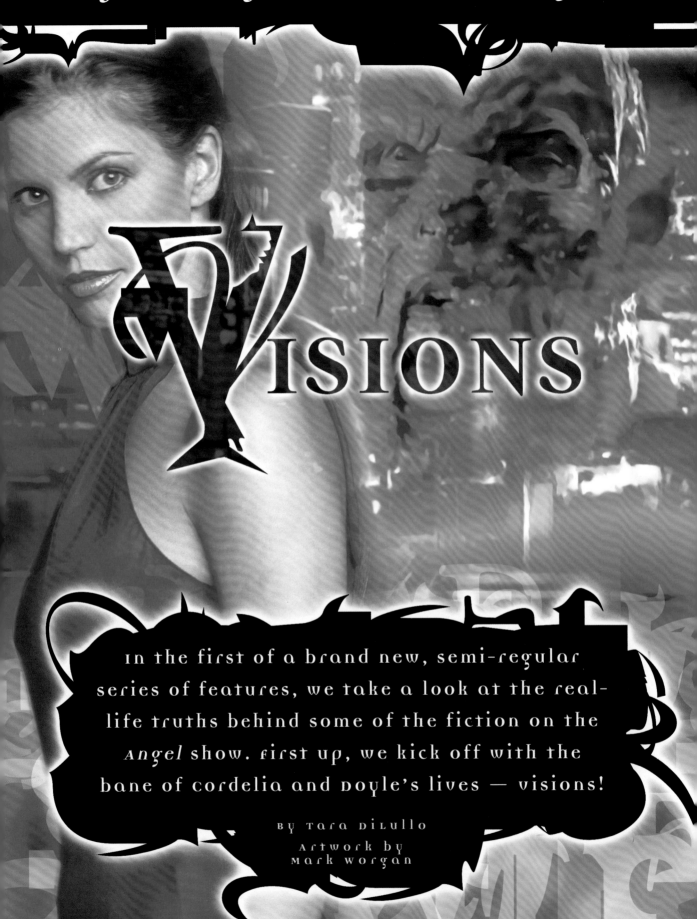

VISIONS

In the first of a brand new, semi-regular series of features, we take a look at the real-life truths behind some of the fiction on the *Angel* show. First up, we kick off with the bane of Cordelia and Doyle's lives — visions!

BY TARA DILULLO
Artwork by
Mark Worgan

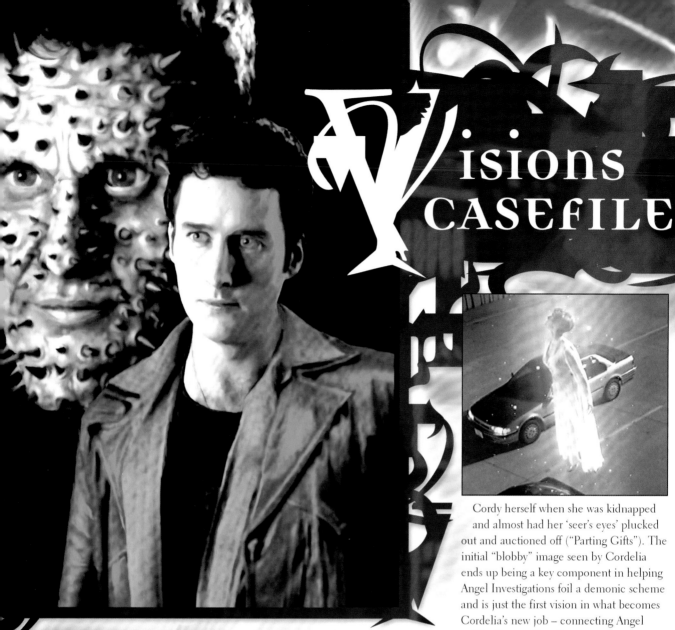

Visions Casefile

Cordy herself when she was kidnapped and almost had her 'seer's eyes' plucked out and auctioned off ("Parting Gifts"). The initial "blobby" image seen by Cordelia ends up being a key component in helping Angel Investigations foil a demonic scheme and is just the first vision in what becomes Cordelia's new job – connecting Angel to The Powers That Be.

case subject:

Cordelia Chase – Female, early 20s, Los Angeles resident with no prior history of telepathic experience.

case history:

Ms. Chase's first vision occurs when she is at a television commercial audition and suddenly a strange image (of "an ugly, gray, blobby thing") appears in her mind, accompanied by excruciating pain. Completely debilitated by the experience, Cordelia eventually understands that the ability to have these visions was passed to her from the demon Doyle, who was given second sight by The Powers That Be. These visions provide Angel with clues that direct him to humans who are in dire need of his help – indeed, the clues once helped Angel rescue

classic definition:

Visions are the mystical experience of seeing as if with the eyes of the supernatural or a supernatural being, according to the American Heritage Dictionary of the English Language.

layman's definition:

Visions are credible images, words, or messages that are received by a person in a supernatural way, which can't be explained by scientific methods or evidence. People who receive these visions are called clairvoyants, psychics, seers, mediums, second-sighted, and telepathic. They will often get glimpses of vital information about a person or occurrence (in any period of time – past, present or future).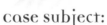

History of Cordelia Chase's visions:

Nov. 30, 1999* – "Heroes": Part demon, Doyle transfers his ability to receive visions to Cordelia through a kiss before he dies.

Dec. 14, 1999 – "Parting Gifts": Cordelia receives her first vision and spends all her time trying to get rid of her 'gift'.

Oct. 10, 2000 – "First Impressions": Cordelia's visions help her save future Angel team member, Charles Gunn.

May 23, 2000 – "To Shanshu in L.A.": The demon Vocah causes Cordelia to experience hundreds of visions, sending her into a coma. On waking, Cordy decides that she must continue to help people, having seen so much suffering in the visions.

Oct. 1, 2001 – "That Vision Thing": Cordelia's visions take on a physical manifestation, which is being caused by a demon brain hacker hired by Wolfram & Hart.

Jan 14, 2002 – "Birthday" Thanks to the visions, Cordelia is diagnosed with widespread neuro-electrical deterioration which puts her in a coma. Cordelia chooses to become part-demon so she can continue to have the visions without them killing her.

May 20, 2002 – "Tomorrow": Because of her powers, Cordelia is chosen to ascend to a higher plane by The Powers That Be.

Oct. 20, 2002 – "The House Always Wins": Cordelia returns to this plane without any memory of her life at the Hyperion or her vision abilities.

Nov. 10, 2002 – "Spin the Bottle": Cordelia's memory is restored and she has a vision of an impending apocalyptic fate.

April 2, 2003 – "Inside Out": It is revealed that Cordelia was maneuvered into inheriting the visions so she could become the vessel of birth for the evil Jasmine. Post-birth, Cordelia slips into a coma.

The Truth Behind the Fiction:

The history of visions throughout the ages is often heavily tied to established religion. As with any phenomena that can't be easily explained with absolute scientific rationalization, visions and people that claim to have the ability to receive messages from the astral planes are either embraced or refuted by society with equal passion.

An early recorded documentation of visions dates back to 1141, when Hildegard of Bingen had a vision of God that gave her the ability to instantly understand the meaning of religious texts. Born the 10th child in a noble family, she was promised to the Catholic Church and lived a cloistered life revolving around religious studies. She founded her own convent, was a prolific composer and wrote a book, Scivias, which detailed her visions of the heavenly world, including some that predicted the course of history. Today some skeptical researchers who have studied her life and the descriptions of her episodes theorize that Hildegard suffered from migraines and that her 'visions' were a side effect – which sounds eerily similar to the experiences of a certain former cheerleader from Sunnydale.

In the Middle Ages, tales of visions became more frequent and individual experiences began to be categorized as either 'divine' – from God – or condemned as a conduit for the Devil and his unholy deeds on earth. How someone's visions were labeled was often determined less by investigation and more by the community or church's attitudes toward the individual.

One of the most famous victims to be caught in the middle of that argument was Joan of Arc. In 1424 at the age of 12, Joan began to have visions of St. Michael the Archangel and Saints Catherine and Margaret. She claimed that she was told by God to lead the French army against the English and Burgundians, which she

eventually did. The Burgundians and English eventually captured Joan, put her on trial for being a heretic and burned her at the stake. History has since revealed that Joan was used as a political pawn by warring rulers, and was not only cleared of the heresy charges after her death, but was declared a saint by the Catholic Church, which in 1920 decreed that her visions were 'divine'.

About 100 years later, one of the best known mediums in all history emerged. In the early 1500s, Nostradamus won repute as a physician and astrologer. He

supposedly 'predicted' future events – including great earthquakes, Hitler's reign, the Fire of London, and World War III – in a series of quatrains (rhyming poems). Nostradamus' biographer and debunker of his works, James Randi, spent years translating the seer's original French works and has never found one world event to definitively match anything Nostradamus predicted. And the rumors that have frequently surfaced on the Internet linking recent events like the World Trade Center tragedy and Osama

Bin Laden to his predictions have all been proven to be false quatrains created after Nostradamus' death in 1566. Regardless of the naysayers, Nostradamus has amassed a vast and loyal following of people who believe the man was a true prophet who received visions of the future, which are continually being revealed.

Over the centuries, the actual origins of visions have been theorized by many but there are some specific categorizes that have come to the forefront. For the faithful, the most popular explanation remains that visions are messages from

God to the seer – period. Those of a more skeptical nature theorize that visions are actually psychotic hallucinations that could be interpreted as visions. In line with that theory is the idea that highly emotional events, such as intense prayer meetings or religious ceremonies, can trigger trances or altered states of consciousness, which create 'vision' experiences in susceptible individuals. And lastly, there is the belief that visions are a supernatural event in which the devil communicates with the seer to control them or pass messages of evil to mankind.

The persecution of witchcraft in the 1600s marked another landmark time for those who experienced visions. The Church began a widespread process of labeling those who admitted to being mediums or having psychic visions as 'witches', and like Joan of Arc, many of them were burned at the stake. There was even an official manual, The Witches Hammer, which helped to guide those seeking to oust 'witches' from the community and world.

Interestingly enough, history has also seen the merging of religion with visionary experiences, resulting in the creation of some of the more contemporary organized religions. George Fox founded the Society of Friends, or Quakers. In 1647, he felt that the voice of God spoke within him and began the Quaker religion based on those messages. Joseph Smith and six of his followers started the Church of Jesus Christ of Latter-day Saints, or Mormons, in the United States during the 1800s. Joseph claimed he was personally visited by two persons of the Holy Trinity who spoke to him in visions and told him to begin a church to share the messages told to him in those experiences. To this day, some Mormons believe that the head of the Mormon Church can receive revelations direct from God, obtained through dreams or waking visions. These are just two examples of religions with visions as part of their foundations that still exist and thrive to this day.

Today, the world of visions and psychics has merged with modern life and has even become a business of sorts, appealing to those who want to know more about the afterlife or what will happen in the future. Psychics have set up storefronts, phone lines and consultation businesses providing a conduit to astral planes through 'visions' and psychic powers for a price. Yet for all the claims, the majority of these new 'mediums' are complete frauds. In response to the need to

separate truth from lies, in the last 60 years a new branch of scientific research has been created to investigate spiritualism and psychic phenomena. Scientist and Professor William Crookes did the first study of spiritual phenomena in his book Researches in the Phenomena of Spiritualism published in 1870. Since then, some noted experts in the field of study have been French psychologist Charles Richet, American psychologist William James and Baron von Schrenck

Notzing. This research is still very much on the fringe of science but is becoming more accepted as the decades progress.

In perhaps the best indicator of mainstreaming of a subject, popular culture has completely embraced the vision phenomenon. From Ghostbusters and Poltergeist on film to the TV shows Touched by an Angel, Miracles and a certain show about a vampire with a soul, visions are often used as a plot device to explore drama as well as the spiritual.

EPISODE SPOTLIGHT

"ARE YOU NOW OR HAVE YOU EVER BEEN"

SEASON TWO
EPISODE TWO

Original U.S. airdate: October 3, 2000 • Original U.K. airdate: January 12, 2001

Synopsis

Angel assigns Cordelia and Wesley to research a mysterious, abandoned Hollywood hotel that closed back in 1979. After piecing together The Hyperion's dark history, they come across an old photograph of Angel from the 1950s and soon discover that their boss has a personal interest in the building. It seems that back in 1952, a detached and reclusive Angel had stayed at The Hyperion. Amidst a series of unexplained deaths at the hotel, a young woman on the run from the police turned to Angel for help. But ultimately her betrayal led to Angel leaving everyone in the hotel at the mercy of a paranoia demon.

Memorable Dialogue

Wesley: "I've been accused of a great many things in my time. But paranoid has never been one of them. Unless people have been saying it behind my back."

Cordelia: "It's kind of like a puzzle. The 'Who died horribly because Angel screwed up 50 years ago?' game."

Angel: "It's been a long time since I've opened a vein, but I'll do it if you pull any more of that Van Helsing Jr. crap with me."

Cordelia: "It's not that vampires don't photograph, it's that they don't photograph well."

Guest Star Info: John Kapelos

John Kapelos was born on March 8 in London, Ontario, Canada. You may not know the name, but the face is instantly recognizable, as John has appeared in over 100 films and TV shows over the course of his career. The prolific Canadian actor made a name for himself in the 1980s, appearing in several John Hughes movies, including *The Breakfast Club*, as well as *Weird Science* and *Sixteen Candles*. He also starred in the cult TV show, *Forever Knight*, and has popped up in numerous TV shows including *Miami Vice*, *L.A. Law*, *The X-Files*, *Frasier*, *Seinfeld*, *ER*, *Quantum Leap*, *Who's the Boss?*, *The West Wing*, and *Queer as Folk*. Recently, he has appeared in *Desperate Housewives* and the movie *Tripping Forward*, alongside none other than *Buffy*'s very own Amber Benson!

Statistics

 No. of times Angel gets his ass kicked : 1

 No. of deaths: 2 (Human), 1 (demon)

 No. of screams: rather a lot

Trivia

A scene at the end of Act One showing Angel as very uncaring and apathetic towards the other guests was cut from the final edit. It featured Angel drinking and turning up the volume of the jazz music he was listening to, whilst the salesman next door committed suicide.

The episode takes its title from a line from the McCarthy era witch-hunt for Communists. During the many trials and inquests of the time, the oft-heard question was, "Are you now or have you ever been a Communist?"

Episode Credits

Written by: Tim Minear
Directed by: David Semel
Angel: David Boreanaz
Cordelia Chase: Charisma Carpenter
Wesley Wyndam-Pryce: Alexis Denisof
Charles Gunn: J. August Richards
Judy Kovacs: Melissa Marsala
Hotel Manager: John Kapelos
Bellman: J.P. Manoux

Denver: Brett Rickaby
Mulvihill: Tommy Hinkley
Actor: Scott Thompson
Salesman: David Kagen
Older Man: Terrence Beasor
Blacklisted Writer: Tom Beyer
Old Judy: Eve Sigall
Thesulac Demon: Tony Amendola

FOLLOWING THE CONCLUSION OF THE FOURTH SEASON, *ANGEL MAGAZINE* CAUGHT UP WITH ACTOR ALEXIS DENISOF FOR A CHAT ABOUT THE LATEST DEVELOPMENTS IN *ANGEL*, AND TO FIND OUT WHAT HE THINKS THE FUTURE HOLDS FOR MR WESLEY WYNDAM-PRYCE.

He may have started out as a bumbling idiot on *Buffy the Vampire Slayer* when he entered the fray as Buffy's new Watcher in Season Three, but Wesley Wyndam-Pryce has since proved himself to be one of the most dangerous men in California. When he first arrived in Joss Whedon's universe, the prissy Watcher barely knew how to hold a stake, let alone face up to a posse of blood-hungry vamps. But Wesley has since stood alongside the Angel Investigations team and faced an endless slew of demons and monsters, even

leading his colleagues headfirst into danger while Angel was otherwise engaged in wreaking his revenge on Wolfram & Hart in the show's second season.

Alexis Denisof is one of the first to admit that the character of Wesley has undergone some significant changes over the years, and reveals that in the early days, he was always trying to persuade Joss Whedon to make his character less of the uptight coward that we all knew him to be. "I always said to Joss that I wanted Wesley to be cool when he was on *Buffy*," he recalls.

"But I like the old Wesley and the new Wesley," Alexis admits, revealing that he has, ironically, particularly enjoyed revisiting the more nerdy aspects of the character in recent

BY

ange

DARRYL CURTIS

episodes of *Buffy* and *Angel* which has seen Wesley take a pounding, and surely one of the character's biggest claims to fame is his ability to have stayed alive against all odds. He's been shot (in "The Thin Dead Line"), had his throat sliced open (in "Sleep Tight"), been almost suffocated by his former boss (in "Forgiving") and tortured nearly to the point of death by Faith (in "Five by Five"). But somehow he's always managed to pull through.

"Joss loves people to suffer, and Wesley has suffered!" Alexis laughs. The actor admits – slightly tongue-in-cheek – that he has always been a little concerned that Joss and the writers might suddenly decide to kill the character off at some point with no prior warning, and has frequently approached Joss for assurance about his future in the show. "Joss told me the room was very divided," he confides, recalling one particular trip to Joss' office to enquire about his future on *Buffy* and *Angel*. "He said, 'Half the writers wanna kill you, and half the writers really want you to survive." Sounds like Alexis didn't exactly get the assurance he was after…

TV show writers and producers often create back stories for the main characters to help the writers and actors better understand and be able to write for and play the characters. These back-stories may never be important to the storyline, but they provide essential colour, without which the characters wouldn't necessarily have the depth and dimension that we see on screen. As Wesley was not a main character but was introduced as a semi-regular halfway through *Buffy*'s third season, no back story existed for him. Therefore, Alexis decided to come up with a background story of his own for his own personal reference, which centred on Wesley's relationship with his father. Not only did this history with Wyndam-Pryce Senior explain to Alexis why the character of Wesley was so repressed, but it

years. "I loved it when Wesley got to be a clown," he says, referring specifically to the *Angel* Season Four episode "Spin the Bottle", in which a spell caused the characters to revert to the personalities of their youth, allowing Alexis to get back into character as he was in *Buffy*.

Another *Angel* episode which allowed Alexis to act the buffoon was Season One's "She", in which Cordelia celebrates moving into her new pad (with Dennis the ghost) by hosting a small soirée for her close friends. As Alexis explains, the script called for Wesley and Angel to dance very badly and fall into people. However, the extras in the episode hadn't been told what was going to happen in the scene, and most of them didn't know who Alexis Denisof was or what his character was like. "People were looking at me, like, 'Who the hell *is* this guy?!'" he recalls. "They didn't know what was going on."

So what does Alexis put Wesley's previously uptight behavior down to? "He needed to get laid!" he laughs. Well, in recent years, Wesley's certainly had his fair

share of female attention. He dated Virginia in *Angel*'s second season, had a brief liaison with a 'bleached blonde' in "Dear Boy", fell head over heels in love with Fred in the third season (although, sadly, as we all know, the feelings were not reciprocated), and had a steamy affair with Lilah in the fourth season. "I've been very lucky with the leading ladies I've had picked for me," Alexis admits gallantly, adding that he didn't expect to be paired with Wolfram & Hart's sexy but dangerous executive following Wesley's alienation from the gang at the end of Season Three. "I was surprised by Wesley and Lilah, but Stephanie's a knockout, so I'm glad he got laid!"

Talking of knockouts, Alexis fondly recalls the climactic fight scene in the *Buffy* episode "Graduation Day", which saw the students taking up arms to join Buffy and the Scooby Gang and helping them bring down the Mayor. Joss Whedon gave Alexis the choice of getting to join in the fray and prove his mettle, or getting knocked out with just one punch. "I chose getting knocked out in one punch for comedic value!" he says.

"Graduation Day" is just one of the

{ "I'M GRATEFUL FOR MY TIME ON *BUFFY* – I MET THE WOMAN OF MY DREAMS THERE." }

also allowed the actor to look at how that relationship – and him facing that relationship – could inform the changes which Wesley has undergone during his time on *Angel*. "I decided that Wesley was internally confronting his father, and that released him a little bit and made him less repressed," he explains. And of course, we eventually did meet Wes' father in this season's seventh episode, "Lineage".

One theme which has been an important part of the *Angel* story of late is the love triangle between Fred, Gunn and Wesley. The friction between Gunn and Wesley has caused some interesting dynamics between the characters, in particular following the events of "Supersymmetry", in which Gunn pushed Fred's self-serving professor to his doom to save her the trouble. Since then, Gunn and Fred's relationship has reached its breaking point, and since Wesley kissed Fred in "Soulless", Gunn and Wesley have practically been at each other's throats. So with Gunn and Fred's relationship now seemingly over, and the obvious chemistry between Wesley and Fred, does Alexis think there's a chance the former Watcher could finally get the girl in the next season of the show?

"I can't say anything about whether Wes and Fred will get together," Alexis says evasively. "I know a few things have been discussed, but nothing is set." As the actor admits, however,

Photo © Albert L. Ortega

Wesley is no longer the love-sick puppy he was back in Season Three, which could make a far more interesting dynamic for a relationship with Fred. "It would be interesting," he affirms. "I could see them together."

While we'll have to wait for Season Five of *Angel* to unfold a bit more to see what kind of romantic liaisons await Wesley, in real life, Alexis Denisof couldn't be happier with his relationship with former *Buffy* co-star Alyson Hannigan. The couple recently got married, and Alexis delights in talking about the relationship, confessing that he is a big Willow fan. The couple, who were firm friends from day one, got together during a trip away with their co-stars. "We just couldn't help ourselves anymore," he says happily, adding, "I'm grateful for my time on *Buffy* – I met the woman of my dreams there."

Alexis is also full of praise for his co-stars on *Angel*, in particular Andy Hallett, who he reveals is the most fun person to have around on the set. "It's not so hard to make Andy laugh, which is one of the reasons I love him so much. Thank God they finally made him a regular."

Props master 'Sparky' is also a favourite on the *Angel* set – partly because he's very ticklish and the cast, especially David Boreanaz, can't help but take advantage of this weakness. "Bless him – he can't control himself when he's tickled. It frightens me because I think he's going to wet himself! But we all love Sparky!"

David Boreanaz may be the eponymous star of *Angel*, but given the events in Season Two, which saw Wesley take on the mantle of leader of the Angel Investigations team, a role that he retained throughout most of the third season, it's not surprising that Alexis Denisof has been asked more than once whether he thinks the show could ever have its name changed to 'Wesley'. So how would he really feel if he were given the chance to be the star of the show? "I'm not sure David would like that," he responds thoughtfully. However, he quickly overcomes his concern for David's feelings. "Who cares what he thinks! I'll call Joss!"

Alexis Denisof recently posed for the latest version of the Wesley action figure, which will hopefully be released from Moore Action Collectibles in 2004. The actor reveals that posing for the doll was a very odd experience. "You have to go and be photographed by this 360-degree laser machine," he explains, doing an impression of how it felt by standing stock still with his arms stretched out by his sides. "It was cool though!" he adds.

It's clear from his enthusiasm about the show and his fondness of his co-stars that Alexis has enjoyed his experiences on *Buffy* and *Angel* so far, and is very happy working on the fifth season of *Angel*. No one knows whether or not this will be the last year, and if the show were to go on beyond a fifth season, if Wesley would still be in it, but the actor admits that beyond his time with Angel Investigations, he does have one particular ambition which he'd like to realise. "Playing Bond would be kind of a dream come true," he says of the quintessential English hero. "Give me two years…"

Thanks to Sean Harry of Starfury Conventions.

Angel Case Files:

Thumbnail Bio:

Former Watcher Wesley was fired by the Council for mishandling two Slayers, then turned rogue demon hunter and joined Angel Investigations. A bookish tag-along at first, he comes into his own as a fighter in "The Ring", and as a leader when he takes charge of Angel Investigations, and leads the rebellion in Pylea. Then the bad guys trick him into betraying Angel, and Wes barely survives attempted murder. He goes out on his own and has an affair with Lilah, but redeems himself by saving Angel from Connor and joining the battle against The Beast.

Best Known For:

Encyclopedic knowledge of all mystic and supernatural literature. If the required information is in an ancient book or manuscript, Wes knows where to find it; if it's in a dead or demonic language, he can read it.

Loves:

Fred and Lilah. Though he doesn't act on his feelings for Fred for a long time, he cares enough about her to be jealous of any man she starts to get close to, like her new assistant, Knox. As for Lilah, Wes may insist he has no feelings for her, but the first thing he does at Wolfram & Hart is try to destroy her eternal contract, to free her ghost from their service ("Home").

Funniest Moment:

Impersonating Angel, Wes does a boomerang act in Bryce's doorway to stop himself from walking in uninvited, then has to chug a glass of fresh blood in front of his host. "Dear God! That's—" (*he manfully suppresses his gag reflex*) – "yummy!" Then he panics at the sight of his reflection, and knocks a sculpture from the wall, jumping away from the mirror. ("Guise Will Be Guise")

Scariest Moment:

Under the influence of the woman-hating empath Billy, Wes becomes a brutal abuser and stalks Fred through the Hyperion, spewing scholarly hate about woman's vileness, treachery, and seductiveness ("Billy").

Don't Ask Him to:

interpret ancient prophecies. First he interprets the Scroll of Aberjian to say that Angel will die ("To Shanshu in LA"). Then he completely buys a false prophecy saying that Angel will feed on baby Connor. His plan to thwart the prophecy by kidnaping Connor plays right into the nasty plans of Holtz and SahJhan, costs Connor the life he should have had, and gives Wes a nasty pain in the neck ("Sleep Tight").

Worst Moment:

Just when he thinks he has rescued Connor from Angel, Wes is ambushed by Justine, who cuts his throat and leaves him bleeding to death, while she takes the baby to Holtz. As he lies on the edge of death, Wes realizes that he has committed an unforgivable betrayal of the people he was trying to save, starting with Angel and Connor ("Sleep Tight").

Moment of Truth:

When Lilah uses him to get to Lorne, Wesley walks out of their relationship with scarcely a word. He can't be with Lilah any more, because he can't let himself be used to hurt his friends, again. ("Slouching Toward Bethlehem") ❧

By K. Stoddard Hayes

WESLEY
WYNDAM-PRYCE

DEATH BECOMES HER

SOME NEWS LEAKED OUT QUITE EARLY ON. JOSS WHEDON WAS GOING TO WRITE AND DIRECT SEASON FIVE'S 15TH EPISODE ("A HOLE IN THE WORLD") AND FRED WAS GOING TO SUFFER A 'SETBACK'. FAN SPECULATION WAS RIFE. WAS SOMETHING GOING TO HAPPEN TO HER PARENTS? WOULD FRED BE INJURED OR CONTRACT A DISEASE? NO ONE COULD HAVE PREDICTED WHAT WAS GOING TO HAPPEN. IN A SHOCKING MOVE, FRED'S GONE (SOB) - HER BODY COMPLETELY TAKEN OVER BY AN ANCIENT EVIL! ACTRESS AMY ACKER DISCUSSES HER CHARACTER'S HUGE TRANSFORMATION AND SHARES HER THOUGHTS ON THE SHOW'S CANCELLATION

By Tara DiLullo

In her three-year tenure as Winifred 'Fred' Burkle, the *Angel* scriptwriters have provided actress Amy Acker with plenty of juicy twists and turns to explore with her quirky character. From slave girl to the head of the Wolfram & Hart Science Division, Fred's evolution, while far from earth-shattering, has definitely been dramatic and frequently touching. So, leave it to Joss Whedon to rip the rug from under Fred and turn her world upside-down in the span of an episode. In "A Hole in the World," the sweet, brainy Texan, who so gracefully came into her own this season, was yanked from this world in a shocking death that rendered fans speechless and more than a little teary-eyed. Amy took a break from shooting Episode 18 to give us the inside scoop on the history of Fred's demise and her new incarnation as Illyria, an Old One reborn.

Still dressed in her Illyria costume, complete with blue hair, Amy relaxes in her trailer revealing when she first learned about Fred's fate. "Joss gave me a little bit of warning last October that it was going to happen. He called me to meet him for coffee and I thought, 'Oh no! Am I in trouble?'" she laughs. "Joss said, 'I'm killing Fred,' and then he didn't say anything for a second and then added, 'But you're still going to be on the show.' I was like, 'Huh?' He explained he wanted me to be this alien princess woman who was very different – the opposite of Fred."

While initially surprised, Amy was also intrigued at the prospect of playing a darker character. "When I was reading Eve's part in 'Conviction', I was like, 'I wish I could be Eve! She's cool!' And then watching Wesley turn bad, I wanted to be cool like him," she smiles. "So, I asked Joss if he would write me a scene or two so I could think of ideas and he did it the next day so I had a few months to think about it. Then he had Alexis [Denisof, Wesley] and I over to his house for dinner and we worked on the new character."

That character, Illyria, literally kills Fred from the inside out, taking over her mortal coil to house the ancient being's life force. Looking like a cross between a blue space alien and an *X-Men* character, Illyria is a far cry from the character Amy is used to playing. "This is probably the most challenging thing I've done just because I was so comfortable playing Fred," Amy shares. "At this point, to do something so different from anything that has been done before on the show had me really nervous. This new character is a big transformation. Fred was always the goofy person hanging out with everyone. Now, I'm very still, with an almost insect-like character that has these weird movements and everything is very foreign to her. I'm still trying to figure it out. The first scene that Joss gave me in October was the first scene we shot of her and I felt very comfortable, but the next time I got new words, I was like, 'I don't know what to do!'" When Amy sought some inspiration from Joss on how to construct Illyria, he gave her an interesting analogy on which to base the character. "His original

thought was he wanted it to be Queen Elizabeth meets the Terminator," she laughs.

Amy continues, "I think it's hard because doing a part for three years, I felt very comfortable coming to work. I felt like I knew where they were going when they wrote something and how it sounded in the writer's head. Like now, if I go on an audition for something else I feel very comfortable doing this Fred thing and it's almost scary doing something different. But having this new character has helped me break that and to remember it's acting and I can do lots of different things. I now remember doing Fred at the beginning was very new and different."

The look of Illyria, with her blue locks, eerie eyes and funky costume, has been one of the biggest helps to Amy in making her character come alive. "Outside of the episode I did in Vegas ['The House Always Wins'] and a little bit of prosthetics, this is by far the most make-up I've had to wear. It's interesting, like if I'm doing rehearsals without the costume and hair and make-up, it feels like I look stupid. But when you have all the stuff on, you become the person, so I think it's great. It's a cool costume. It took us a while to get it so it wouldn't break every time I sat down. I'd move around and it would crack all over. It's a unitard that has all this different stitched stuff all over it."

As for the make-up effects, Amy says she

has an earlier make-up call now, but she still gets off easier than Andy Hallett (Lorne). "I only need two hours [to put it on], but I'm not a morning person," she laughs. "Still, nothing is too bad and it's nice make-up, which is easy to get on and off. It was supposed to fade more, but they decided they like it like this." She does add that initially they spray-painted her own hair blue, which took seven washings to get clean, but she still stained her sheets and pillowcases blue each night. "Now I have a wig," she chuckles.

Considering her deep fondness and attachment to Fred, Amy was okay with letting Fred go, mostly because Joss was the one to write and direct her swansong episode. "We were so lucky because Joss was supposed to do Episode 22 and then some stuff came up and he had to pull out, so Alexis and I asked if he would do 15 ['A Hole in the World']. Joss said he couldn't and we kept calling him for three weeks asking, 'What if you did do it? Seriously'. And then the day before Christmas, he called saying, 'Merry Christmas! I'm doing 15'. So having him do that last episode with Fred felt good and being able to work with Alexis was great. We had a whole day that was the hardest day I've had on the show. We were crying for like 12 hours. Joss pushed us farther and I felt he knew what Alexis and I were able to do, so he made us go a lot farther

{ "[PLAYING ILLYRIA] IS A BIG TRANSFORMATION. JOSS' ORIGINAL THOUGHT WAS HE WANTED IT TO BE QUEEN ELIZABETH MEETS THE TERMINATOR." }

than we would have with someone else who would be willing to accept less. It was so hard and emotionally draining, but if it hadn't had been that way, I would have been uncomfortable about that being the end of [Fred]."

Amy does share one small regret in that Fred and Wesley's just burgeoning relationship ended so quickly. "I knew that with Joss he wasn't going to let us be together for long. Their relationship was something Alexis and I hoped would happen so we would get more scenes together, and it seemed like it was meant to happen, but then I didn't think it would be as short as it turned out. Three years for that!" she laughs. Yet Amy is pleased that Wes and Illyria are still tied together in the final episodes of Season Five. "I think Wes is able to see Fred in Illyria and I think the only reason he lets her stay around is because he has hopes Fred will come back. Illyria uses that to her advantage and then somehow finds a loyalty to him and uses him to help find her place."

Amy also confirms that Fred truly is dead, as they revealed in "Shells". "If we had another season, I would have been Illyria, not Fred. Joss talked about doing

some stuff where she was almost like a Superman/Clark Kent type thing, where they would switch personas so more of Fred would come out in her over time. It sounded really interesting, but now that we have such limited time left that probably won't happen." But Amy does add that we haven't seen the last of Fred yet on *Angel*. "Luckily, last episode I did a flashback to Fred and I think there will be a couple more, so I'm getting to do both characters. They are so different and when I did the Fred flashback the other day the whole crew said, 'We're so glad Fred is back! She's so much nicer than the other girl!' she laughs adding, "Fred is so much more like who I am."

Reflecting on the other major changes of the season, prior to Fred's death, Amy has nothing but positive things to say about the fifth season, including Fred's glam makeover. "I liked Fred

TOP 10 FRED

GONE BUT NOT FORGOTTEN – HERE IS OUR PICK OF THE VERY BEST FRED EPISODES:

"Over the Rainbow"
(Season Two, Episode 20)
Despite glimpses of Fred in "Belonging", this is Fred's proper first appearance, as an ex-'cow' on Pylea.

"Fredless"
(Season Three, Episode Five)
Fred's parents visit L.A. – will she go back home with them?

"Billy"
(Season Three, Episode Six)
Gunn and Wes go psycho, and Fred's left alone at the Hyperion with them…

"Provider"
(Season Three, Episode 12)
A demon race turn to Fred for help solving a strange puzzle.

"Waiting in the Wings"
(Season Three, Episode 13)
Team Angel head to the ballet, and Fred gets a new love interest.

"The House Always Wins"
(Season Four, Episode Three)
Fred and the gang need to rescue Lorne in Las Vegas.

"Supersymmetry"
(Season Four, Episode Five)
Fred discovers the truth behind her trip to Pylea, and her relationship with Gunn reaches a turning point.

"The Magic Bullet"
(Season Four, Episode 19)
Jasmine's slowly taking over Los Angeles – and Fred's the only person who hasn't been brainwashed!

"Smile Time"
(Season Five, Episode 14)
Fred and Wes finally get it together!

"A Hole in the World"
(Season Five, Episode 15)
Tragedy strikes Wolfram & Hart, after a mysterious sarcophagus turns up at Fred's lab.

in jeans and a T-shirt and tennis shoes, but they called me before the season started and said they wanted to make Fred more sexy and flirty in how she dresses. It was fun for me because it was different. Normally in my life, I wear jeans and T-shirts, so I was getting to dress differently and I could mention to the costumers, 'Oh, I really like [designer] Betsy Johnson,'" she laughs.

As for Fred's shiny new lab, Amy was also pleased to spend a good bulk of the season among the beakers and microscopes. "We spent a lot more time there than I thought we would. They built the set and it was a cool place that wasn't office space. It seems like a lot of cool stuff and intimate scenes have gotten to happen there. I loved the episode 'Hell Bound' and the scenes with James [Marsters, Spike] in the lab. I hardly knew him at all and it was exciting because I felt very comfortable as I sort of was like Fred with him. I ended up liking him in the same way she liked him."

While she missed working with Charisma Carpenter (Cordelia) throughout the season, Amy was happy to get to know the new women on the show, Mercedes McNabb (Harmony) and Sarah Thompson (Eve). "It was exciting because Mercedes is really funny and it's nice to get a comic girl to work with. 'Harm's Way' was a lot of fun. Sarah is great too and I like having both of them around. I never got to work with Julie Benz [Darla], but we have always had these strong recurring female characters like Lilah [Stephanie Romanov]. It's fun to have these actors around so much that they feel like they are part of the show."

Sadly, the news of *Angel*'s cancellation broke two weeks before this interview, and the cast and crew were all still reeling from the news. "After we found out that the show was canceled, I was really upset and I was talking to my husband and he said, 'You have to realize the show was on for five years and most shows aren't on that long.' I know that, but coming here feels like the best job ever. It's a job, but it never felt like it was going to end because we all love being around one another and there never was any weird tension. We came here and everyone was always professional and working towards the same goal, so it was a little bit shocking."

Amy adds that she definitely felt there was another season left in the series. "I heard all of the ideas Joss had for next season and I just started doing this new character and I feel like I'm barely understanding where it's going to go. I'm still trying out new things every episode, so I was excited to have another year because I felt like there were a lot of stories left to tell. The show this year clicked and it was fun being able to do things like the puppet episode ['Smile Time']. It was unexpected and sad but David [Boreanaz] and James and Alexis have been all been doing the same characters for seven years, which is a lot longer than my three years."

Reflecting back on those three years, Amy is grateful for the variety the series has afforded her. "When I first auditioned for the part, it was a different character. Her name was Logan and she was a librarian. Then I met with Joss and David Greenwalt and we talked. I'm from Texas and somehow it came out that I liked Mexican food and all of a sudden I get the script, and now, it was this girl from Texas named Fred that liked Mexican food, so they put me in there. I always played the ingénue roles and it was really exciting for me to play this character who was quirky but hides a bigger personality. I feel like I've become more like her in my real life over the years."

Amy continues: "We were putting together a reel of different clips from the show recently and one of my friends was watching and asked, 'How many shows have you been on?' and I laughed, 'No, that's all the same person.' I really have gotten to do a bunch of different stuff on the show. It's great having such good writers and Joss and all of these people who want to stretch you and have you try new things. As soon as you say, 'I don't think I can do something,' they are the first people to try to make you do it. It's been fun."

As to what Amy's future holds now that the show is coming to a close, she isn't really sure yet. "I really like working on TV for nine months a year and then having a sum- mer. I had a good time on the show and I'd love the opportunity to do this again someday. There are a million people who want to do anything in TV and that's how I feel. If I can get any job, I would be happy, but it will be hard because this one has been so great. There are so many shows out there that are good, but they don't have the levels this show has every episode. It will be a lot different. I'd like to audition for some things because I haven't for three years. It's time to start exercising that muscle again!"

Asked about the possibility of returning to make *Angel* movies for The WB next year, Amy isn't sure yet. "The only thing I heard was a possible movie. Hopefully, what Joss said about everyone having other jobs will be true. But, I think it would be fun because you always say, 'Oh, we'll keep in touch, and you never know if you will. So, I would do it in a heartbeat if they asked me to."

For the immediate future, Amy's place will be on the *Angel* set finishing the last episodes. "It's always in the back of your head now, but we are all still trying to do our best for the writers and Joss." She hopes that the legacy of the show continues on long after the last episode. "I hope people will always remember it and with the DVDs continue to enjoy it." She adds with a shy smile: "The show is so human, but filled with all these demons, and it's exciting to be on a show that people care that much about." 🦇

> "I KNEW THAT JOSS WASN'T GOING TO LET [FRED AND WESLEY] BE TOGETHER FOR LONG. THEIR RELATIONSHIP WAS SOMETHING ALEXIS AND I HOPED WOULD HAPPEN, BUT THEN I DIDN'T THINK IT WOULD BE AS SHORT AS IT TURNED OUT. THREE YEARS FOR THAT!"

ANGEL CASE FILES:

THUMBNAIL BIO:

Fred grew up in Texas with her loving parents, Roger and Trish. She was a brilliant physics student until her mentor, Professor Seidel, got jealous of her genius and sent her to Pylea, through a dimensional portal. After surviving there for five years as an escaped slave, she was rescued by Angel and his friends. She joined Angel Investigations (after weeks of hiding in her room), where she has helped kick butt, research complex problems and have an affair with Gunn. Her greatest accomplishment may be finding and firing the magic bullet that saves Team Angel from Jasmine's spell.

BEST KNOWN FOR:

Brains. Such good ones that when a bunch of Lubber Demons need a new head for their Prince, they pick Fred's, because she solves the complex mathematical puzzle that is their test ("Provider").

LOVES:

Math and physics, Wesley (?), ice cream, Knox (?), tacos, popcorn (not necessarily in that order).

THE GUY MAGNET:

Who'd have picked the brainy, bespectacled "Texas twig" (Lilah's words) to trigger the rivalry of two hot guys like Gunn and Wesley?

THE MACGYVER OF ANGEL INVESTIGATIONS:

Fred likes to build things – bizarre, ingenious contraptions made of whatever is handy, like the battle-axe launcher (or it might be a toaster?) she builds in the hotel lobby, which is great for decapitating demons ("Fredless"); and the elaborate booby trap she springs on the Billy-fied Wesley ("Billy").

DANCING WITH DESTINY:

Fred's parents think her home in Texas is the best place to recover from her ordeal in Pylea – until she solves team Angel's bug mystery. Professor Seidel urges her (however hypocritically) to return to physics, where she could make a real mark with her knowledge of dimensional portals. But Fred knows that her experiences have made that life impossible. Instead, she's the perfect candidate for a new career: head of scientific research at Wolfram & Hart.

FUNNIEST FRED IMITATION:

Lilah in glasses and pigtails, asking Wes if it turns him on to think of Fred and promising in a Southern accent, that if she's a good girl and eats all her vegetables, she might someday have hips ("Apocalypse Now-ish").

WORST MOMENT:

Fred's contact with Jasmine's blood breaks Jasmine's spell, allowing her to see the radiant Goddess as a maggot infested demon. Fred flees from the Hyperion, pursued by her closest friends. She escapes Wes, Gunn, and even Angel and Connor. But just when she thinks she's safe, complete strangers turn to stare at her and speak in Jasmine's voice. Fred realizes that Jasmine is in every single person she meets and can see her wherever she tries to hide ("Magic Bullet").

DON'T ASK HER TO:

Forgive a betrayal. Especially the kind of betrayal that sends her to a Hell Dimension for five years of terror and misery. When she realizes that Professor Seidel has sent numerous other students through demonic portals and tried to murder her not once, but three times, she plans her revenge. Her answer to her friends' advice that vengeance changes everything, and that she'll have to live with her actions for the rest of her life, is, "He's a serial killer."

MOMENT OF TRUTH:

Fred means to take revenge alone, because she doesn't want Gunn to share the guilt of murder. He tries to talk her out of it, but at the last minute, he breaks Seidel's neck and throws him into the portal so that Fred won't have to bear the guilt. Weeks later, a simple conversation about a bath forces the two to face the fact that their love affair is over. Fred planned a murder, Gunn carried it out, and it stands between them like a wall. ❤

BY K. STODDARD HAYES

WINIFRED BURKLE, A.K.A FRED

SEASON THREE EPISODE FIVE

"FREDLESS"

Original U.S. airdate: October 22, 2001

Synopsis

Searching for their daughter who has been missing for five years, Roger and Trish Burkle turn up at the Hyperion Hotel. It immediately transpires that their daughter is in fact Fred. But the unexpected visit from her parents causes Fred to panic and run away. Whilst she walks the streets of L.A. alone, Team Angel tries desperately to figure out what caused the newest member of the gang to run away. Angel, Wes and Gunn split up to search for Fred.

Eventually, they find Fred and she breaks down; everything that's happened to her finally taking its toll. Her parents take to the fact that Angel is a vampire who fights demons like water off a duck's back. They are just happy to discover their beloved daughter safe and out of harm's way. Believing she has no place in L.A., Fred prepares to go home with her parents. But after she saves Angel from an insect demon, Fred realizes that her home is with Angel and the gang.

Memorable Dialogue

Cordelia: "(Imitating Buffy.) Oh, Angel. I know that I am a Slayer, and you're a vampire and it would be impossible for us to be together, but…"
Wesley: (Imitating Angel.) "But... my gypsy curse sometimes prevents me from seeing the truth. Oh Buffy..."
Cordelia: "Yes, Angel?"
Wesley: "I love you so much I almost forgot to brood."
Cordelia: "And just because I sent you to Hell that one time doesn't mean that we can't just be friends."

Guest Star Info: Gary Grubbs

Born on November 14, in Amory, Mississippi, Gary Grubbs has notched up a prolific acting career since leaving Mississippi for Los Angels in 1977. He kick started his acting career with guest starring roles in the likes of cult shows The Dukes of Hazzard and Charlie's Angels. With more than 50 notable TV appearances to his name, Gary appeared in some of the 80's most popular TV shows, including Hill Street Blues, Happy Days, The A-Team, Magnum, P.I. and L.A. Law. He has also popped up in ER, The X-Files and Will & Grace. On the big screen, Gary has appeared in JFK, Runaway Jury and, most recently, Ray. The actor now resides in Hattiesburg, Mississippi with his wife and two children.

Statistics

 No. of times Angel kicks ass: 2   No. of deaths: 2   No. of screams: 1

Trivia

- This episode marks the first appearance of Fred's parents, Roger and Trish Burkle.
- In an earlier version of the script, Fred's family was larger, incorporating two brothers and a sister.
- Jennifer Griffin has appeared on Six Feet Under and The X-Files. Her movie credits include A Perfect World and Vanilla Sky.

Episode Credits

Written by:	Mere Smith	Winifred Burkle:	Amy Acker
Directed by:	Marita Grabiak	Lorne:	Andy Hallett
Angel:	David Boreanaz	Roger Burkle:	Gary Grubbs
Cordelia Chase:	Charisma Carpenter	Trish Burkle:	Jennifer Griffin
Wesley Wyndam-Pryce:	Alexis Denisof		
Charles Gunn:	J. August Richards		

[L
W

EGAL EAPON

IT'S ALL NEW FOR GUNN IN *ANGEL* SEASON FIVE – NEW THREADS, NEW ATTITUDE AND A NEW SINISTER SIDE TO HIS PERSONALITY... ACTOR J. AUGUST RICHARDS TALKS US THROUGH THE CHANGES.

J. August Richards is feeling the love. It's been four-plus years since he joined the cast of *Angel*, assuming the role of street-smart warrior Charles Gunn. The character, at first, lent the Angel Investigations team a healthy dose of extra muscle, which came in handy whenever the crew took on demons or vamps or zombies. But what could have been a clichéd character, what might have been a short-term recurring role, evolved into something special.

As the episodes and seasons passed by, the writers developed other facets of Gunn. He made friends and enemies, and also lovers, mainly in the form of Fred. He revealed his humor and his self-doubts and even his vulnerability; at times he seemed more humbled by the lingering affections between Wesley and Fred than any fanged foe he faced in the darkened alleyways of Los Angeles. *Angel* fans quickly took to Gunn and also to J.'s finely tuned and affecting performances. He's a favorite guest at conventions around the world, a friendly and accessible guy who welcomes the opportunity to make a personal connection with the audience.

And now it's on to Season Five of *Angel*, which finds Gunn at the top of his game, armed with an ungodly amount of knowledge about the law, sporting nifty suits and operating as a full-fledged member of Angel's team as they seek to keep a lid on evil by working from within LA's breeding ground of evil, the law offices of Wolfram & Hart. *Angel Magazine* caught up with J. on a rare morning off, as the actor made a pitstop at a coffee shop and then, properly energised by a caffeine pick-me-up, set about updating

Angel readers on his off-season exploits, looking back at Season Four of the show and previewing what promises to be an entertaining Year Five.

ANGEL MAGAZINE: LET'S START WITH YOUR SUMMER HIATUS. WHAT WERE YOU UP TO BETWEEN THE END OF SEASON FOUR AND THE BEGINNING OF THIS SEASON?
J. AUGUST RICHARDS: What did I do this hiatus? I basically took the whole summer off. I recorded a lot of music. I wrote a bunch of songs with a friend and was exploring that aspect of my creativity. I honestly don't know if anyone will ever get to hear it. I love music, but right now it's just a hobby for me. I don't really have professional aspirations musically at the moment. It's another outlet for me, another way to express myself.

What else did I do? I went to Europe. I went to another convention in Europe and then I spent some time there just chilling out there. Then my family came to visit me, and the next thing I knew I looked up and my hiatus was over. That's the way it happens. We have such a short amount of time off, so that was basically everything I did.

THE INTERNET MOVIE DATABASE STATES THAT YOU WERE IN A RECENT TELEVISION MOVIE CALLED *CRITICAL ASSEMBLY.* IS THAT THE ONE YOU DID THAT WAS ORIGINALLY CALLED *GROUND ZERO*?
Yes, that aired this summer. I did that with a couple of other actors

from the WB, but it aired on NBC. I did it with Kerr Smith from *Dawson's Creek* and Katherine Heigl from *Roswell* and a really great Canadian actor named Jeff Roop. We played college students who were nuclear arms activists. It was more or less about terrorism. We'd shot it a long time ago, but it wasn't ever able to air because of the political climate. It was called *Ground Zero* when we shot it, and we obviously had to change the name [following the events of September 11, 2001, in the US]. So that aired this past summer and it was almost like they had to sneak it on the air because it just wasn't the right time to be airing a television movie about four college students building a nuclear bomb. But I think the film turned out really well and I had a great time doing

{ "YOU CAN'T FORGET THAT UNDERNEATH THE SUIT [GUNN] IS STILL AN INCREDIBLE WARRIOR. I LOVE THAT THIS GUY CAN WEAR A SUIT AND STILL FIGHT. I LOVE WHAT GUNN'S BECOME AS A CHARACTER." }

it. The new title was a term used in building nuclear bombs, but I'm sure it meant nothing to the general public.

OKAY, LET'S SWITCH TO *ANGEL*. LOOKING BACK ON SEASON FOUR, WHAT WOULD YOU SAY WE LEARNED ABOUT GUNN THAT WAS NEW AND IMPORTANT?

The most interesting thing was that I spent a lot of the episodes talking about how I was trying to find my place and feeling like I was just the muscle in the group. Gunn was, in a lot of ways, trying to find his place and in "Players" he got a lot of validation from Gwen Raiden and from what she was asking him to do. So I think that Gunn really found himself in that episode and even more so in the season finale ["Home"]. When we got to the end, to the finale, and Wolfram & Hart made him this offer, this sort of silent offer, Gunn was really clear about the fact that he wanted to take it.

WERE YOU SATISFIED WITH THE WAY THE DEMISE OF THE GUNN-FRED RELATIONSHIP WAS HANDLED LAST SEASON? SOME PEOPLE THOUGHT IT WAS A LITTLE ABRUPT AND DIDN'T PROVIDE ENOUGH

EMOTIONAL PAY-OFF. WHAT ARE YOUR THOUGHTS?

In some ways it was disappointing for me because I love working with Amy so closely. So in some ways it seemed that we broke up and dealt with it sporadically. I felt like I did miss a final reconciliation or a final sense of closure on the relationship. That's what I would say so far as how our relationship came to an end.

THE WB CERTAINLY SURPRISED A LOT OF PEOPLE AFTER SEASON FOUR CONCLUDED. THEY PICKED UP *ANGEL* FOR A FIFTH SEASON, PLUS THEY BROUGHT JAMES MARSTERS ON BOARD AS SPIKE AND HANDED THE SHOW AN AMAZING TIMESLOT, RIGHT

GREAT RESPONSIBILITY." SO, WHAT DOES ALL THAT MEAN FOR GUNN?

The drawback for Gunn is that nobody on the team trusts him entirely anymore. Everybody feels that I should not have done it, that something may have been stuck in my brain when I got all the legal information that I was not aware of, that will cause me to do something bad at some point. So I feel that the gang doesn't trust me, but what I created for myself in the fourth-season finale was the idea that Gunn is sick and tired of feeling so powerless. All of his life and ever since we met him on the show he's been fighting tooth and nail, putting two sticks [together] to make a weapon out of it. And now, for the first time in his life, he wants some juice, he wants some power, and he's happy to have that. He's

  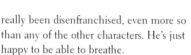

AFTER *SMALLVILLE*. HOW PSYCHED WERE YOU, AND HOW PSYCHED WAS EVERYONE ELSE?

Everyone was completely psyched because we knew the show was going to take a major change. It was going to be more of an episodic structure. So, after coming off a season in which every episode fed into the next, we were looking forward to doing a season where each episode pretty much stood alone. And I personally was excited about James joining the show. Working with him the little bit I got to work with him at [one of] the Shakespeare readings at Joss' house I was excited to see what he'd bring to the table on *Angel*. I have to say that he's a dynamic actor and he's a great addition to the cast.

DAVID BOREANAZ HAS SAID THAT HE WELCOMES THE LATEST CHANGES ON *ANGEL*, BUT THAT FOR THE CHARACTERS IT'S A MATTER OF BE CAREFUL WHAT YOU WISH FOR. THEY WANTED TO BE ABLE TO FIGHT EVIL AND NOW THEY'VE GOT EVERYTHING AT THEIR FINGERTIPS TO DO SO. BUT AS A VERY DEAD RELATIVE OF SPIDER-MAN ONCE SAID, "WITH GREAT POWER COMES

really been disenfranchised, even more so than any of the other characters. He's just happy to be able to breathe.

GUNN'S NOW TAKEN TO WEARING A SUIT. CONSIDERING WHERE HE'S BEEN AND THE NUMBER OF TIMES WE'VE SEEN HIM SOAKED IN BLOOD, THAT'S GOT TO BE QUITE A CHANGE OF PACE FOR YOU, RIGHT?

It's wonderfully strange. (*Laughs*) I think that from the "Players" episode and from the ballet episode ["Waiting in the Wings"], Gunn feels completely comfortable all dressed up. It's just another aspect of who he is, but what's most interesting to me is that you can't forget that underneath the suit this guy is still an incredible warrior. He's still ready to fight if he has to. So I love that this guy can wear a suit and still fight. I love what Gunn's become as a character.

HAVE YOU SHOT ANY GUNN-HEAVY EPISODES YET FOR THE NEW SEASON?

The first episode ["Conviction"] is probably the most Gunn-heavy episode of them all so far this season. You got to

see how he got the power that he has now. So that was his biggest stuff so far. We're just finishing Episode Six now and, as usual, any story or character developments just come as a surprise to me and to everyone else. Joss doesn't tell us a lot in advance and I actually hate to be given previews of what's going to happen. Sometimes they'll give us a preview and it doesn't happen, and you've gone and gotten excited about it. So, at this point, I just like to read the script when I get it and be surprised along with everyone. Also, just because an episode isn't Gunn-heavy that doesn't mean I'm not busy. I'm in every episode and I'm chasing baddies with a gun or an axe in my hand. And I love fighting in my suit. Fighting in a suit is really kind of comfortable. It comes naturally to me. I'm more of a dressy person in real life, so I think Gunn in a suit, even if he's fighting, is a little closer to who I am.

NOW THAT *BUFFY* IS OFF THE AIR AND FIREFLY IS NO MORE, WORD

SARAH THOMPSON ARE ADDING AS, RESPECTIVELY, HARMONY AND EVE? Poor Amy is the only female regular in the cast now, so it's nice to have a little more oestrogen around. So just from that aspect it's good to have Mercedes and Sarah on the show. Mercedes is just the funniest thing in the world. That girl is hilarious and she makes every one of her lines hilarious. Sarah is incorporating into the cast quite nicely and I love working with her. Gunn trusts no one, especially vampires. He's a lot like me in that respect. It takes me a while to trust someone implicitly and especially in a life and death circumstance. Gunn's got all of that and he's on the enemy's turf. So he doesn't know what to make of Spike yet. He really doesn't.

YOU'RE VERY MUCH INVOLVED WITH THE SHOW AWAY FROM THE CAMERAS. YOU'VE GOT AN OFFICIAL WEBSITE. YOU APPEAR AT CONVENTIONS, MOST RECENTLY SHOWS IN LONDON AND

"I PERSONALLY WAS EXCITED ABOUT JAMES [MARSTERS] JOINING THE SHOW. I WAS EXCITED TO SEE WHAT HE'D BRING TO THE TABLE ON *ANGEL*. HE'S A DYNAMIC ACTOR AND HE'S A GREAT ADDITION TO THE CAST."

IS THAT JOSS WHEDON HAS BEEN A MUCH MORE VISIBLE PRESENCE ON THE *ANGEL* SET. HOW ACCURATE A STATEMENT IS THAT?
Joss has been making his appearances. We were very happy to start the season with him directing the first episode. That was great. He really pushes you as an actor. At the end of the episode I have to give this huge courtroom speech and that was the first scene shot for the season, and it was shot at six o'clock in the morning. Anybody who knows me knows that before 10am I can be walking around, but I'm not really awake until 10am. So it was a very difficult scenario for me. But it was fun working with him. He forced me to wake up and was constantly giving me notes about different ways to play my scenes.

CAN YOU TALK A LITTLE BIT MORE ABOUT THE ADDITION OF JAMES MARSTERS TO THE SHOW AND ALSO ABOUT WHAT MERCEDES McNAB AND

AUSTRALIA. WHAT'S BEHIND ALL THAT?
That's all part of the experience. One experience I had that really touched me was that the first fan letter I ever got after coming onto *Angel* was from a guy in England. I'd gotten some fan mail before, but this was the very first piece of fan mail in relation to this show. So I got the letter and I wrote him a letter myself and thanked him for the kind things he'd said in his letter. I then met him when I went to London and I've seen him again since I've been back. So it's really cool to connect with people in that way, with people who really like the show. I've really enjoyed the conventions I've been to in the past few years. I've met some really interesting people. They're so kind. They give me gifts that they know I'll like because they've read about my liking it in some interview or heard me mention it at a previous convention appearance.
And that's great.

FOUR-PLUS YEARS IN, IT SEEMS LIKE YOU'RE STILL HAVING A GOOD TIME. SO, ARE YOU STILL HAVING FUN?
I am still having a good time because the show is always changing, and the character is always changing. I love the fact that sometimes when I'm at work I get nervous, and that's because I'm being asked to do something new. It's not like I'm doing the same thing every week that I've done since the beginning. It's always something different, whether it's getting overcome by some strange spell or putting on a suit or having a relationship with Fred. It's always something different for me to play and that keeps me excited and interested and on my toes. I like being nervous about going to work and being nervous about what I'm going to do next.

J. AUGUST RICHARDS, THANK YOU VERY MUCH! ❦

BY Kate Anderson

THE WAYS OF THE GUN

AS SOME KIND OF URBAN ROBIN HOOD, SELF-APPOINTED SLAYER OF VAMPIRES – CHARLES GUNN – MADE IT HIS MISSION IN LIFE TO KEEP THE STREETS SAFE. HIS STREET-SMART ATTITUDE AND FIGHTING SPIRIT MADE HIM A FORCE TO BE RECKONED WITH, AND IN TURN, GUNN PROVIDED US WITH MANY A MEMO-RABLE MOMENT. HERE'S OUR COUNT-DOWN OF FIVE OF 'EM.

5. Killing for Fred

The episode: "Supersymmetry," Season Four, Episode Five

What happens: Gunn accompanies Fred when she is asked to make a presentation at the Physics Institute. But Fred bumps into her old professor, Dr. Seidel, and is shocked to discover that he was responsible for sending her to Pylea.

Why it's so memorable: Who'd have thought we'd see the shy, sensitive Fred on a road trip of revenge?! Events take a shocking turn when Gunn does the dirty deed for his beloved and gets rid of the nasty professor. Well, they do say love makes you do the strangest things. But Gunn committing such an act is comp. in conflict with his code of ethics.

1. From street hood to hot shot lawyer

The episode: "Conviction," Season Five, Episode One

What happens: Team Angel take charge of the L.A. branch of evil law firm Wolfram & Hart, and Gunn takes the Senior Partners up on their offer to enhance his mind with a comprehensive knowledge of the law.

Why it's so memorable: As a young man who sees he has much unused potential, Gunn is seemingly willing to do whatever it takes to become as far removed from being seen as just the brawn of the group as possible. But despite being a (very) questionable choice, it's fair to say Gunn cuts a fine figure in his designer suits.

3. The last stand

The episode: "Not Fade Away," Season Five, Episode 22

What happens: It's time for Team Angel to bring down the powerful Circle of the Black Thorn. And it's a fight that could well be the last – for everyone. Gunn is given the task of taking out the evil Senator Brucker and her vampire minions, which results in him being seriously wounded.

Why it's so memorable: Charles Gunn comes full circle and he's a redeemed man. Gone are the smart suits and the briefcase. This is a job for the old Gunn; the street smart vigilante who's more used to a fist fight than a courtroom battle. And in typical Gunn, pig-headed fashion, he's not gonna let the fact that he's seriously wounded – possibly fatally wounded – stop him from fighting on. Go, Gunn!

1. Dusting Alonna

The episode: "War Zone," Season One, Episode 20

What happens: A gang of youths, led by the streetwise Charles Gunn, patrols a not-so-safe area of L.A. Determined to rid the streets of the unwanted night crawlers, Gunn is contemptuous about the whole idea of a 'good' vampire like Angel.

Why it's so memorable: Gunn's first episode includes the pivotal moment that was to make the vigilante sit up and question his motives. Dusting vampires became rather matter-of-fact for Gunn – until his sister was turned into the very thing he hated the most, and he was forced to dust the one person he cared most about.

2. Showdown with an old pal

The episode: "That Old Gang of Mine," Season Three, Episode Three

What happens: It seems Gunn's old crew are back in the demon hunting business and are creating a rather bloody trail in the process. And not only do they view their former commander-in-chief as a traitor, but they want to reduce Angel to dust, too. No longer Mr.

Why it's so memorable: Poor old Gunn. No longer Mr. Emotionless, his loyalties are completely torn. Does he side with his old chums, or stick with his new friends? Sometimes there is a gray area between good and evil, and Gunn's situation is a perfect example. It's not always so black and white. Plus, the whole hostage situation – with guns! – is very in your face.

10 THINGS YOU NEVER KNEW ABOUT...
j AUGUST RICHARDS

1 J August Richards was born Jamie Augusto Richards III on August 28, in Washington, DC. Raised in the Maryland suburb of Bladensburg, he was the first American-born child in his Panamanian family. At the tender age of 14, he changed his name because no one outside of his family could pronounce it correctly!

2 J. discovered his passion for acting at an early age. He enrolled in a performing arts high school and began appearing in several plays a year. He applied to only one college – the University of Southern California – and was not only accepted, but he also won numerous scholarships and grants to study theater. Whilst attending USC, he met George Hertzberg and Danny Strong (*Buffy*'s Adam and Jonathan) who were enrolled at the same time. To this day, George remains one of J.'s closest friends.

3 J.'s family was slightly surprised by his career choice. His parents weren't too happy when he announced his decision to become an actor. In fact, his mum always wanted him to be a lawyer – or a priest!

4 In his spare time, J. enjoys painting – although he admits he's not particularly good at it! He also has a keen interest in astronomy.

5 Aside from *Angel*, J.'s small screen appearances include *The West Wing*, *Chicago Hope*, *The Practice*, *Sliders*, *Space: Above and Beyond*, and *The Cosby Show*. His movie credits include *Why Do Fools Fall in Love*, *Good Burger* and the TV movie *The Temptations*. Most recently, he appeared in the action drama *Critical Assembly*, alongside Kerr (*Dawson's Creek*) Smith and Katherine (*Roswell*) Heigl.

6 To prepare for the role of Charles Gunn, J. didn't have to look too far. A friend with whom he plays chess is very similar to the character, so he just picked his brain. J. loves doing research – so much so, his friends say he has an obsessive-compulsive disorder when it comes to his work!

7 For J., one of the coolest things about working on *Angel* is the fight scenes. "I dig kicking those evil booties," he says.

8 The lucky lady in J.'s life is fellow actress Tangi Miller, who is probably best known for her role in the hit TV series *Felicity*. Tangi, alongside Alyson Hannigan and *Charmed* star Holly Marie Combs, was a spokesperson for breast cancer.

9 One of J.'s favourite ever roles was that of Taj Mahal in the Mark Taper Forum production *Space*. He played a rapper and bike messenger who thought he was possessed by aliens. It was one of the funniest roles of his career.

10 J. claims to have something of a Spidey sense! "I can't count the number of times something strange has happened to me," he says. "I have Spidey sense all night and day. It amazes my friends sometimes because I can tell so much about people in the instant I meet them."

Compiled by Kate Anderson

THAT OL' DEVIL CALLED

Lorne

Apparently, it's not easy being green. Well tell that to Andy Hallett who is having an absolute blast playing Lorne the Host of Angel! We spoke to the lively actor to find out what's in store for everyone's favorite demonic singing sensation!

From his first appearance in the *Buffy* universe as one of Professor Maggie Walsh's students (at the start of "Hush"), to his scene-stealing moments as The Host of Caritas (a.k.a., Krevlorneswath of the Deathwok Clan, as his own people will persist in referring to him), Andy Hallett has been having a ball. The karaoke bar host who has an insight into the psyches of those who sing around him has steadily increased in importance through *Angel*'s most recent seasons to the point where he is pretty much a part of the team itself.

Andy Hallett followed his dream to become an actor and whenever he's talking at conventions or in interviews, he emphasises how blessed and lucky he feels to be on *Angel*. During the hiatus between the third and fourth seasons of *Angel*, Hallett travelled the world with his co-star and buddy, Mark Lutz (who plays the Groosalugg), touching down in Great Britain for a 10-day stopover. We caught up with him as he journeyed between convention appearances...

*Interview
by Paul Simpson*

WHAT'S DOWN THE LINE FOR THE HOST IN SEASON FOUR? ARE WE GOING TO SEE THE HOST IN LOVE?

ANDY HALLETT: I don't know. That would be fun. What would happen? You can pretty much do anything – literally anything – on this show. My head was cut off and put back on. I would love to see him in love – it would be fun to have a little romance for the Host. I don't know what it would be: human or demon or something else, but it would definitely be a trip for sure.

AFTER THE SUCCESS OF BUFFY'S MUSICAL EXTRAVAGANZA "ONCE MORE, WITH FEELING," WHAT ARE THE CHANCES OF A MUSICAL EPISODE OF ANGEL?

I would love to do one. When J. August Richards and I came out of the premiere of the *Buffy* musical, we thought that we should do an *Angel* one. We weren't even praising Joss like everyone else was – eventually of course we told him it was wonderful – but when we first walked out of the theater, with both of us being such hams, and both having a love for music, we looked at each other and said "*Angel*. Musical." It's not on the cards, but it would be great if it was.

> "YOU CAN PRETTY MUCH DO ANYTHING – LITERALLY ANYTHING – ON THIS SHOW. MY HEAD WAS CUT OFF AND PUT BACK ON!"

ANY TALK OF GOING ACROSS TO BUFFY THIS SEASON?
No, not to my knowledge.

WOULD YOU LIKE TO MAKE THE TRIP TO SUNNYDALE?
Oh yes, I'd love to.

WHAT DID YOU THINK OF ANGEL'S SEASON THREE CLIFFHANGER?
It was great. It fits the description of cliffhanger in every sense of the word. The Host goes to Vegas, which I think is hilarious. It's the perfect spot for him, if you're going to send

him anywhere apart from L.A. Angel's sinking to the bottom of the ocean in a box, Cordelia's floating up to heaven, and the Groosalugg goes off to fight crime. It's a real cliffhanger, because it leaves you hanging going, "Are any of them coming back? Will there be a show? What's happening here?"

To be totally honest, I never know what's going to happen next. They don't even tell us very much. Those guys in the production office, and especially Joss, are very serious about being tight-lipped. When information leaks out they don't like that at all. They like everything to be suspenseful and a surprise for everybody. That's what makes the shows a great success. Every episode, people are just stunned.

WHAT WAS YOUR HIGHLIGHT OF SEASON THREE?

Believe it or not, working with the babies who played the new-born Connor. That was really interesting for me. *Angel* has been my first professional acting gig, and I feel that on this show we have such a diverse cast – not so much in terms of the regular castmembers, but in terms of the guest cast and some of the people who

appear from week to week. I've had the pleasure of working with old and young, experienced and inexperienced – all different types. But the one thing that I didn't have any experience of was working with babies. There are actually three babies that we used on the show: They're triplets and one of them really is called Connor. They turned out to be really funny and incredible. They were terrific.

WHAT WERE THE SPECIFIC PROBLEMS INVOLVED WITH WORKING WITH BABIES?

When the babies are on set, it's pretty serious because there are so many rules surrounding

what you can and cannot do with them there. According to the Screen Actors Guild regulations, you have to have the babies in and out of there within something like 22 minutes, so when you do a scene with one of them, you have got to know your lines. You've got to be ready to go. When they come in, there's not much time.

SO IT'S AS TECHNICAL AS WORKING WITH AN UNREPEATABLE SPECIAL EFFECT?

Exactly. So that gave me extra motivation to do the scenes. I'll never forget a scene at the end of "Provider" where Fred is tied up, and Cordelia walks in with baby Connor in her hand. It was this really powerful moment where Cordy stops the Prince and the Prince's minions from cutting off Fred's head. And she's walked into the room with this live, gorgeous baby boy. Of course, I was tied up on the floor, which is a whole other story – sounds like a typical weekend! – and I'm looking up at her. Of course Charisma always looks fantastic, but when she walked in, she seemed so powerful and elegant, yet at the same time she had this baby in her arms. For some reason that really hit me, and afterwards she and I started talking about how really amazing it was to work with these babies. It gives you this huge motivation to get the scenes done.

The babies always have a massive entourage. Their entourage is probably bigger than the one Diana Ross has. They've got a nurse, a care provider, a baby-sitter type person, and normally one of their parents there as well. It's amazing how many people you need to look after these babies.

THE GREEN *Mile*

Andy Hallett discusses his criminal experiences!

"My dad taught me to drive when I was eight years old on a 1980 Toyota pick-up truck. I grew up driving tractors, lawn mowers, ATVs, motorcycles: every type of vehicle you can imagine. I bought myself a school bus when I was 13 years old. A 33.5' long, bright yellow school bus! This guy knew my dad, and said he'd give it to me for $500. I had $502 in my bank account so I cleared that out. My Dad was looking at it like it was his kid's first investment. Forget stocks and bonds – let's buy buses. He knew that if I bought it for $500 we could turn it around in a couple of months and make some money on it. I bought it as an investment, but I ended up falling in love with it.

"My bus was the talk of the town – it was on the cover of the front page of our local newspaper. I had it for about a year and a half. Then one night I sneaked out with it. I come from a place called Osterville, MN, which is a tiny sleepy town. At 8pm, the sidewalks roll up. I thought, I've never got my frigging bus out of second gear – I'm out of here! So I took it out, down the street to the development where my friends lived, and picked up a half a dozen of them. You can picture me backing into their driveways – all of a sudden they heard the beep of the back-up alarm of my bus! Everyone had thought I would pick them up in the ATV. I had half a dozen kids in my bus, and we were roaming around the neighborhood. We did emergency evacuations out the back door, we pulled over with the stop sign out. We just had a ball.

"But don't you know it? Somebody, and I don't know who, called the cops on me and said 'Andy Hallett is out in his school bus and it's unregistered and unlicensed. You need to get him!' The cops were waiting at the end of my driveway. They asked me a few questions, and then they arrested me. I got cuffed and taken to jail at 14 years old. I was appalled. My mother and father were more appalled than I was. My mother couldn't believe it, and my dad really couldn't believe it. When I was sitting in this little holding cell at the police department, the officer came over after half an hour and said, 'We've notified your parents and I've got good news and bad news.' I said, 'Give me the bad news first.' 'Your dad was just here to pick you up, and he was about halfway to get you then he said he was too pissed off to even lay eyes on you and he said to find your own way home. The good news, we called your mum and she's on her way to get you.' I knew I was so in trouble."

Transcribed by Paul Simpson

completely genuine. I guess he was reacting to Andy, not the Host.

No, it didn't frighten them, but before you handled the babies, you had to wash your hands. The nurse that was with them would come up with hand sanitizer and make you do that. That was a bitch for me, because it wiped the make-up off my hands. My make-up artist got pissed when I wiped the make-up off! It's not as if anyone was going to be doing a close-up on your hands. That's what I'd tell him – "I'll hold the baby from the back. You'll never see my palms, promise."

YOU ALWAYS SEEM TO GET KNOCKED OUT IN THE FIGHTS – WOULD YOU LIKE THE CHANCE TO GET DOWN AND DIRTY?

[Boreanaz] and I had done a bunch of scenes together before then, but this time we were out in the car. We were driving in the convertible – well, really of course we were being towed by the *Angel* crew – at 1am on a Friday night. We were driving through downtown L.A., and people were coming out of the bars, recognizing David and myself and yelling out at us. Even if they didn't recognize us, seeing a car being towed around with a bunch of cameras and a green guy in the passenger seat would turn anyone's head, I would suppose – or it'd make you think you were totally screwed up.

In one scene, demons attacked us in the car, and I had to get out. Basically, the Host gets his way out of trouble by trying to hit a high note and scaring off the other people, which is totally nuts and insane and crazy to do on-set. The fights are wonderful and fun, and we have a great

{ "I JUST LOVE GETTING A CHANCE TO MEET WITH THE VIEWERS. I LOVE HEARING WHAT THEY HAVE TO SAY, I REALLY DO." }

HOW DID YOU FIND WORKING WITH THE CONNOR BABIES ON YOUR OWN?

I loved it. In "Waiting in the Wings" I was working with the baby, singing him lullabies. It was probably the most real moment I'll ever experience on that set. I was baby-sitting while the others went off to the ballet, and I sang that gorgeous lullaby with all those nice words. However, at the beginning of that lullaby I was singing the regular tune, and while I was putting him in the crib, the baby was screaming. Then once I'd put him down and I started really singing to him, he stopped! He was staring me in the eye as I was singing to him. That was by far the most real, authentic moment that I had on the show and it blew me away. I try really hard to be genuine and authentic in all my scenes, but that's the first time where I've actually done something and got exactly the effect I was looking for. It was

I'd love to. I always think it's funny when my character has a fight scene. The Host is not a fighter – he's a lover, not a fighter. He's a lounge guy with a drink in his hand; he's certainly not a fighter. I'll never forget when they gave me my very first fight scene. It was in Season Two's "Happy Anniversary." That was my first time getting out of Caritas, going out with the gang and fighting crime with Angel. I had a ball. I really enjoyed it. It was another one of my favorite moments. David

stunt co-ordinator, Mike Massa. He is so great: he just works so hard, and every fight scene is so well choreographed. He puts so much time and energy into everything he does. Of course, when I have a fight scene, my stunt guy has to look just like me, so he has to go through three hours of make-up too. If I'm in a fight it's quite a big deal.

WHAT WAS YOUR FAVORITE FIGHT FROM THE THIRD SEASON?

I like that last one I got into, when Wesley beat me up. He threw me over the desk, then started whaling on me, and hit me over the head with the trophy. That was so funny for Alexis and I. We laughed so hard and he was making so many jokes. When the camera was over his shoulder – looking over his back and giving me my close-up – Alexis was telling

jokes as he was punching me in the face. "This is like a night with your girlfriend!" Whack! Whack! Whack! Of course, I couldn't laugh because the camera was in my face. He's nuts – I love Alexis.

DO YOU FOLLOW *BUFFY* AND *ANGEL* NOW ON TV? ARE THEY THE SORT OF PROGRAMS YOU WATCH FOR PLEASURE?
I hadn't before I got this gig, but now I do. It's always so interesting to watch my friends on TV and think that I hang out with them. When we're together, J. and I will be talking about where we want to go to eat, or the usual things friends talk about. Then I tune in and there he is, doing a great job on national television. I always like seeing my friends working.

YOU'VE SPENT PART OF THE SUMMER TRAVELING ROUND THE WORLD WITH MARK LUTZ PROMOTING *ANGEL*. WHAT'S THAT BEEN LIKE?
We've been having a fantastic time. Going to conventions is a whole lot of fun. We've done small scale ones and big ones. The one in London was a pretty decent sized one. I just love getting a chance to meet with the viewers. I love hearing what they have to say, I really do. If people are willing to come out to see us, then I'm very happy to spend time with them. After all, if they don't watch the show, I don't have a job!

ANDY HALLETT, THANK YOU VERY MUCH.✛

Angel Idol

We all know that **The Host** is a top quality entertainer, but just how well have the other *Angel* characters performed in their karaoke stints at Caritas? The *Angel Special* team have made a sudden – some might say, irrational – decision to leave the world of publishing, and enter the slightly more lucrative music industry – so let the judging commence! Your panel: 'Nasty' Martin 'US Editor' Eden, Marcus 'Designer' Scudamore and Darryl 'UK Editor' Curtis!

Harmony
Song: "The Way We Were"
Episode: "Disharmony"
Martin: "I think I've gone deaf. Or maybe I just wish I had."
Marcus: "The episode title says it all..."
Darryl: "Ten out of ten for effort!"

Angel
Song: "Mandy"
Episode: "Judgement"
Martin: "Great brooding quality... a few singing lessons might help..."
Marcus: "Nerves probably got the better of him on the night, but he has definitely got soul."
Darryl: "I think this guy might be tone deaf..."

Darla
Song: "Ill Wind"
Episode: "The Trial"
Martin: "Beautiful! This Darla girl is amazing! Sign her up now! What? What do you mean she's dead?!?!"
Marcus: "The girl's good, but I can't see much of a future for her."
Darryl: "That's really brought tears to my eyes! What a star performance!"

Liz the Lizard Demon
Song: "I'm so Excited!"
Episode: "Judgement"
Martin: "He has star quality, but unfortunately, I think he picked the wrong song..."
Marcus: "His heart's in it, but his vocals aren't."
Darryl: "His enthusiasm is infectious! I'm so excit- uh, sorry..."

Mordar the Bentback
Song: "Sexual Healing"
Episode: "Judgement"
Martin: "Very funny!"
Marcus: "He's got the whole Barry White thing going on. I like it!"
Darryl: "Um..."

Durthock the Child Eater
Song: "Achey Breaky Heart"
Episode: "Judgement"
Martin: "I can't actually hear his voice..."
Marcus: "Maybe it's telepathic karaoke?!"
Darryl: "Next!"

Kane
Song: "L.A."
Episode: "Dead End"
Martin: "Is this guy really a lawyer?!"
Marcus: "Put your hands together for Lindsey! (Geddit? 'Hands' together...)"
Darryl: "Amazing – especially considering the recent hand transplant. This man has talent."

Fred
Song: "Crazy"
Episode: "That Old Gang of Mine"
Martin: "This sounds like her first attempt at karaoke – a shaky start, but room for improvement."
Marcus: "Very sweet but that doesn't always get you places in this game. Sorry."
Darryl: "Send her back to Pylea!"

Cordy, Wesley, and Gunn
Song: "We are the Champions"
Episode: "Redefinition"
Martin: "I've heard worse. Oh, hang on... I haven't."
Marcus: "This one's my favorite – there's so much love in the room!"
Darryl: "'Rescue Me' might have been a better choice of song..."✛

Lorne's Guide To Karaoke

LORNE'S DO'S AND DON'TS

Whatever your musical talents, there was no finer place to give the old vocal cords an airing than Caritas. It was the hippest, hottest karaoke bar this side of the galaxy – and it had an added bonus, too: Lorne! Caritas' affable Host would work his magic and read your aura – if you wanted to know what the future had in store for you, all you had to do was pick a song, step up to the microphone and belt out your favorite tune. Of course, these days Caritas is sadly no more. So, as a tribute to our favorite karaoke bar, we've put together a few karaoke do's and don'ts...

DO MAKE EVERYONE FEEL WELCOME

At Caritas, everyone was invited. And by everyone we mean *everyone*! As karaoke bars go, they didn't come any cooler than Caritas. Here you'd find humans mingling alongside demons, vampires and even worse – lawyers! It didn't matter what your religion, color or creed, you'd always be made to feel most welcome by Lorne, the host-with-the-mostest. If you were seeking a little enlightenment, you couldn't have found a better place.

DON'T BE A TROUBLEMAKER

Violence is a definite no-no – no matter how bad someone's singing may be. And Caritas was (usually) a violence-free environment, thanks to a sanctorium spell placed by The Transuding Furies. Troublemakers would not be tolerated, under any circumstances. Which meant no concealed weapons, no fighting and certainly no eating the clientele.

DON'T GET EMBARRASSED IF YOU CAN'T SING

Remember that embarrassment is just a state of mind. It doesn't matter whether you've got the voice of an angel or a voice that could break glass. Angel may have massacred 'Mandy', but he still managed to survive the experience – just! And Sonny and Cher's 'I Got You Babe' by the two Japanese businessmen was so awful it was hilarious. Although the least said about Harmony's rendition of Barbara Streisand's 'The Way We Were' the better! But the truth is, no one really cares whether you can sing like an American Idol. It's the taking part that matters.

DO MAKE SURE YOU PICK THE RIGHT SONG

When it comes to karaoke, it's an open mike. So pretty much anything goes. Whether it be Motown classics, Barry Manilow, Madonna or JLo, the choice is yours. You may choose to follow in the Host's (green) footsteps with an oldie but goodie. 'I Will Survive', 'Superstition' and 'Lady

HIGHS AND LOWS

Caritas has seen some great performances – and some too excruciating, even for demon ears! Here's just a few of our favorites – and ones we'd much rather forget...

LOWS

Angel – 'Mandy';
Durthock the Childeater – 'Achy Breaky Heart';
Mordar the Bentback – 'Sexual Healing';
The Japanese businessmen – 'I Got You Babe';
Harmony – 'The Way We Were'

HIGHS

The Host – 'Lady Marmalade';
Lindsey McDonald – 'L.A. Song';
The Lizard Demon – 'I'm So Excited';
Darla – 'Ill Wind (You're Blowin' Me No Good)';
Angel and Connor – 'Jasmine' (so bad it's good – well, almost!)

Marmalade' are always crowd-pleasers. Or if you're brave enough, you could even go one better and perform your own song! After all, it worked well for that nasty Lindsey McDonald. When he was on stage singing, he seemed almost human!

DON'T INTERRUPT A SINGER WHEN PERFORMING

Interrupting a singer is a cardinal sin - no matter how bad their performance may be. It takes a lot of guts to get up on that stage. So, shouting, booing, and negative comments are not encouraged. Neither is joining in with someone's song – unless invited to do so. Remember, we're all here for the same reason – to have a few drinks, sing a song and have a good time. ✨

Pop Angel

EVER WONDERED HOW ANGEL AND CO. WOULD FARE IF THEY TOOK PART IN AMERICAN IDOL? AND MORE IMPORTANTLY, WHAT SONGS WOULD THEY SING? WELL, WONDER NO LONGER! AFTER MUCH THOUGHT AND DELIBERATION, WE'VE COME UP WITH THE PERFECT TUNES...

ANGEL – 'HERO' BY ENRIQUE IGLESIAS

Okay, so maybe Angel's 'vocal talents' aren't in the same league as the Latino heartthrob's. But anyone would feel a little weak at the knees listening to Angel sing this romantic power ballad. Hmm, on second thoughts, maybe not!

This Cat Stevens' classic couldn't be more appropriate for Cordy. Angel and Connor. Do we really need to say more?

GUNN – 'BEAT IT'

These days, Gunn may look the city slicker in his fancy suits, but he'll always be the street-savvy demon hunter to us. And to fit in with his old gang image, what could be better than this Michael Jackson classic.

FRED – 'IT'S RAINING MEN' BY THE WEATHER GIRLS

What with both Gunn and Wesley vying for her attentions, Fred's certainly not short of admirers!

LORNE – 'I CAN SEE CLEARLY NOW' BY JOHNNY NASH

Let's face it, whatever Lorne sings, it'll be brilliant. Simon Cowell would be climbing over himself to sign our favorite big green guy, that's for sure!

WESLEY – 'I'M YOUR MAN'

We can just picture Wes belting out this Wham classic. Of course, we all know which lady he'll be thinking of when he's singing, don't we? (No, not Lilah!)

SPIKE – 'REBEL YELL' BY BILLY IDOL

The bleached blond hair; the leather coat; the attitude... These two guys have a lot in common – apart from the vampire thing!

LILAH – 'BITCH' BY MEREDITH BROOKS

Nuff said! ✨

Angel Magazine's (very) Rough Guide to Pylea

DREAMING OF A MUCH-NEED-ED BREAK? PERHAPS YOU AND YOUR SIGNIFICANT OTHER JUST CAN'T AGREE WHERE TO JET OFF TO FOR YOUR ANNUAL HOLI-DAY THIS YEAR. WELL, HOW ABOUT SOMETHING A BIT DIFFERENT? IF YOU FANCY AN ALTERNATIVE TO THE USUAL SUN, SEA AND ER, SIGHT-SEEING, THEN *ANGEL MAGAZINE* HAS GOT JUST *THE* PERFECT DESTI-NATION IN MIND... HOME OF LORNE — PYLEA!

BY KATE ANDERSON, WITH MARTIN EDEN

COMMUNICATION

Most of Pylea's population speak English as a language, so you shouldn't have any problem communicating with the locals. However, written language does not use vowels, so reading Pylean literature aloud may prove embarrassing. Rudimentary dancing can also be used as a method of communication. Popular choices include the Dance Of Joy (performed by the Krevlorneswath clan when Lorne disappeared from Pylea) and the Dance Of Honor (used to, er, honor people). Let's not talk about the Dance Of Shame, however...

A BRIEF HISTORY

Pylea is home to a variety of different races, including humans, demons and Hairy Hell Beasts. For a long time, humans were looked upon as the lowest of all species – and treated as such. It has a ruling class of pink-skinned priest-demons and was traditionally a very black-and-white world. When the Groosalugg recently became Pylea's new ruler, a democratic government was established, making it a much safer place to travel to – until Groo carelessly got ousted...

GETTING THERE

Forget flying or catching a train, when it comes to traveling between worlds, getting there isn't quite that simple – but then, that's half the fun! Visiting an alternative dimension like Pylea can only be done via a natural gateway – otherwise known as a portal or "a big swirly hole". Certain geographical areas are rife with psychic energy, and these function as dimensional hotspots. However, a word of warning: if you're traveling in a party, not everyone who goes through a portal together always ends up in the same place. You certainly wouldn't want to lose your interfering mother-in-law, now would you...?

ADVICE FOR VISITORS

Xenophobia (nothing to do with Xena) is pretty much the watch-word in these parts, so don't be offended if the locals don't initially welcome you with open arms. It's probably best not to do anything to attract too much atten-tion, such as experience a painful/blinding vision in the middle of a street or start singing show-tunes. Just play it low key and keep your head down – if you want to keep it!

THE DANCE OF JOY: AN EASY, STEP-BY-STEP GUIDE

1. The preliminary jig. Lift left leg (bending at the knee), then repeat with opposite leg.
2. Now lift the whole left leg to a 90-degree angle. Repeat with the right leg.
3. Lurch dramatically towards the left, arms aloft.
4. Leap into the air, arms waving. Almost Snoopy Dance-esque, except sideways.
5. Now the difficult bit. Jiggle around from side to side, tapping your head with both hands.

LOCALS

The Covenant of Trombli was a force to be reckoned with in Pylea. Made up of crimson-robed
priests, the rather inconsiderate head, Silas, once
ruled with racial and religious persecution.
Humans – usually referred to as 'cows' – were
kept for hard labor and treated as slaves, which
didn't exactly do much for their self-esteem.
Other members of Pylean society include
floppy-skinned, miserable pink people and
green-skinned demons, much like Lorne –
but minus the snappy dress sense!

WEATHER

In terms of climate, Pylea is very similar to
Earth. In fact, if anything, the weather
can be decidedly warmer, thanks to the
added bonus of Pylea having not one but
two suns! Yep, that's right. So don't forget
to pack the shades and plenty of sun-
screen. Pylea is also very vamp friendly.
Vampires can walk in the sunlight, and
even see their reflection. Word of warning
to vampires, however: going into full
vamp mode will bring out the *real*
demon in you – and you could end up
slaughtering your nearest and dearest.

CUSTOMS

One of Pylea's greatest honors is The Bach-nal.
This ritual killing involves swinging a ceremonial
axe, known as the Crebbil, usually to sever your
head from your body before feasting on your
remains. Yes indeedy, Pylea loves its customs,
and cutting people's heads off appears to be a
popular form of execution. For Lorne, the biggest
down-point of his trip back home was, without
question, being ridiculed and decapitated – a
traditional welcome home celebration with party
poppers and balloons would have been much
more appropriate.

FOOD & DRINK

Pyleans love their food. They often hold village feasts, where locals get together to tell stories and feast on, um, humans! They also enjoy the odd tipple. Flib liquor is a popular choice, and a lot of drinking is done at The Hall of Drink and Chance (try saying that when you've had one too many Flibs…).

WHAT TO DO

Pylea is a very primitive world. Forget nightclubs, casinos, fine dining or even the theater. But they do have on offer the likes of jousting, where you can enjoy a good old-fashioned combat with lances. Alternatively, you could try a spot of drokken-hunting, which is an ancient tradition. And since Pylea's landscape is not dissimilar to our own, you could always take in some fresh air and go for a nice ramble. Just, y'know, watch out for those drokkens.

ENTERTAINMENT

Fighting, fighting and more fighting. Pyleans do enjoy watching a good rumble, and watching the Groosalugg do battle always attracts big crowds. Music, however, is a completely different story. To say Pyleans don't have a love of music would be something of an understatement. Music simply doesn't exist. Similarly, singing is frowned upon in a *big* way. In fact, it seems to be regarded as a form of torture on Pylea. So, remember: if you ever need to make a demon moan and scream out in pain, try singing it a tune. It seems to work on Simon Cowell…

News

BY EDWARD GROSS

ANGEL IS NOW OFFICIALLY OVER (BARRING ANY POTENTIAL TV MOVIES) WHICH MEANS WE'RE BIDDING A FOND FAREWELL TO SOME CHARACTERS WE'VE GROWN TO LOVE OVER THE YEARS. WE CATCH UP WITH JAMES MARSTERS TO FIND OUT WHAT IT'S LIKE SAYING GOODBYE TO MR. BLONDIE BEAR HIMSELF, SPIKE.

INTERVIEW WITH AN VAMPIRE

As disappointing as the cancellation of *Angel* has been, the one thing that can be said about the series is that it's gone out a creative winner, with cast and crew firing on all cylinders and the fanbase desperate for more.

Although it hardly needs to be pointed out, Season Five of *Angel* was marked by the addition of James Marsters as Spike to the cast, which in many ways reinvigorated the character dynamics and the show itself – which is saying a lot about a series that didn't particularly need reinvigorating in the first place.

At the time of the following interview with

James, he had just completed shooting a sequence for Episode 21, "Power Play". Although he doesn't detail the specifics of the scene, the obvious excitement he feels proves, without a doubt, that this is an actor who would have had absolutely no problem in continuing to portray Spike.

ANGEL MAGAZINE: I'VE GOT TO TELL YOU, YOU SOUND ABSOLUTELY GIDDY. WHAT THE HECK WENT ON OUT THERE?
JAMES MARSTERS: Every now and then, everything the actors want to have happen

every day comes to pass. Sometimes it gets frustrating because you have things that you want to try, but there isn't time or money, so oftentimes you don't get what you want to do. But this was a very pivotal scene in the 21st episode – I don't want to talk about what it was, but it needed to have a really high commitment from everybody, emotionally. It's one of those scenes that could have just been phoned in, it could have been a scene that was like a lot of others, but we have a good director and David [Boreanaz] just drove the train – speech after speech after speech, and he just *brought it*. All of us who were basically just watching him, we could have phoned it in, but sometimes it all works [laughs]. So often an actor is moment to moment, but to have their commitment so high that you're lifted… that's why I became an actor. David is a really good actor. He's one of the few actors that I can honestly just look at and not throw them off. Oftentimes when I just look at somebody and say, "Hi, how are you doing?", it can throw off what they're planning to do. David is the kind of actor who's just there in the moment, and whatever happens just kind of happens. That makes for really good television. I think what the camera's wanting to see is the actual event; something happening for the first time and not something that's recreated. The only way to get to that is improvization, and David can do that. It's just fabulous [laughs]. David and I and Gunn and Wes – we only had a couple of lines, but we were so locked with each other. A lesser director wouldn't have given us the full take. They would have let us say the one line so we could cut into it. But Angel is trying to convince us to all do something that is hard to ask. So it really was a scene about whether he could do that or not.

WHO'S THE DIRECTOR?
James Contner. Love that man! He has always been one of the best directors. A really steady hand. He helped shoot *Jaws*, so he's done it and he just has a way of knowing where to put the camera, first of all; how to frame a little wonderful shot and when you edit enough really pretty pictures together, it starts to look like a movie. He's just very good at what he does without calling attention to himself. Yesterday, going into the scene, there was a shot that had to happen at the end of the scene, a special effects shot, and we were pretty much getting scrunched into the position of having to decide where we were going to end up in the scene without having actually done the scene yet. Oftentimes in television you have to bow to that, but James just figured out a way to rework this very crucial shot on the fly and give us the option to come and rehearse the scenes and do it fresh in the morning. The benefit of that is just astronomical. Before that, David Greenwalt came in to direct an episode and I was feeling that, between these two directors, I was ready to do another 22.

I REMEMBER WATCHING "SHELLS" AND THINKING AFTERWARDS, "AND THIS SHOW IS CANCELED, WHY?!" THE TWO-PART EPISODE WAS SO MOVING AND SO UNLIKE ANYTHING ON TV. AND TO HAVE YOU BE SO BUZZED ABOUT EPISODE 21 – THE CANCELLATION IS JUST SO FRUSTRATING.
It's okay. It's over, man. I'm from the theater, so we're used to it.

BUT YOU'RE GOING THROUGH THIS FOR THE SECOND TIME, FOLLOWING THE END OF *BUFFY*.
Yeah, but by the time *Buffy* was over, I was pretty sure I would be coming over to *Angel*.

WAS THE EXPERIENCE OF THIS SEASON AS GOOD AS YOU HOPED IT WOULD BE AT THE BEGINNING OF THE YEAR?
It was much better than I thought it would be. I mean, I thought it would be fine, but it turned out to be fabulous. The cast is just fabulous. They're all just such hard workers; none of us whine and actors can tend to do that and it rolls. You have one person who whines a lot, and sooner or later everyone does. But David has a real commitment that's impressive. He really wants it to be good, he's not coasting at all. I wasn't prepared for that.

"[JOINING *ANGEL* HAS BEEN] MUCH BETTER THAN I THOUGHT IT WOULD BE. I THOUGHT IT WOULD BE FINE, BUT IT TURNED OUT TO BE FABULOUS. THE CAST IS JUST FABULOUS."

DID YOU HAVE A DIFFERENT PERCEPTION OF WHAT IT WOULD BE LIKE?

I know what television is, I know what can happen and I know what the workload can do to a person and how tempting it is to relax a bit, especially after you've played a character for six years. It takes a very inquisitive mind to keep exploring your character after six years – and that's what he's done.

ARE YOU READY TO LEAVE SPIKE BEHIND? HAVE YOU PLAYED HIM LONG ENOUGH THAT THE BREAK ISN'T THAT PAINFUL?

If a project was offered to me that was cool and had Spike in it, I would love to do it. It's a fabulous character, but at the same time, it seems to be over so it's a good time to move on. I've been in the business long enough that you don't walk away from something that's humming, that's working. I don't walk away from that.

SO IF THE SHOW WAS COMING BACK FOR A SIXTH SEASON, YOU WOULDN'T HAVE A PROBLEM WITH IT.

Assuming the larger components were the same. At the same time, I'm excited about playing other characters. Frankly, I can't wait to show the world my brown hair, and the fact that I don't have an English accent and the fact that I don't have to be the snarky guy all the time. Thankfully I have enough money that I can kind of pursue what I want; I don't *have* to take something right away. You can actually start to think in terms of having a career as opposed to paying the rent, which is the best thing you could hope for.

BETWEEN BUFFY'S LAST SEASON AND THIS YEAR ON ANGEL, HOW WOULD YOU SAY THAT SPIKE HAS EVOLVED?

He's no longer an asshole, though he doesn't give a crap what people think of him. In fact, I'm arguing with one of the producers about a line. I said, "You want the old Spike, but that's not the same guy." The

thing is he's not at war with the world or with himself anymore. He's starting to see things clearly; he's starting to see what is important and what's not important. So it's a very deep change on the inside. He can actually care about people and trying to help them, and that is just a profound change as opposed to basically enjoying ripping up everything around him. At the same time, Spike is a faker. He's not really a tough guy, he's the biggest poser in the world. He was actually this little poet but then he got turned into a vampire and quickly discovered that he could pose

as the toughest guy in the whole world and get away with it, because he was indestructible. He just took that personality on and it felt good, so he kept it so long as it would become him. That personality works for him, and just because he's decided to help

the world, doesn't mean he's going to drop it. So on the outside it's very much the same, but on the inside he's just entirely different.

YET AT THE SAME TIME, IN ONE OF THE EPISODES HE HAD ABSOLUTELY NO PROBLEM IN TORTURING INFORMATION OUT OF SOMEONE. IT'S GREAT THAT HE CAN SLIP INTO THAT MODE IF HE HAS TO.

Oh yeah [*laughs*]. He's driven by a lesser of two evils at that point. I also think that Buffy, given those circumstances, would have dirtied her hands as well. There comes a time when even that is appropriate. There's a time for everything. It's also fun to play that because that's when Spike can allow himself to go enjoy hurting someone. He can allow himself all the joy of the kill, but morally he can only enjoy that when it's an evil person he has to take care of. Which is really a very wonderful place for him to be, because he can actually kill off evil with his hands, which most of us can't do.

THERE WAS ALSO A MOMENT DURING THE SEASON WHERE ANGEL TRIED TO SYMPATHIZE WITH A BADDIE BY NOTING THAT HE WAS AN INNOCENT VICTIM, AND SPIKE RESPONDS, "SO WERE WE... ONCE UPON A TIME."

That's a profound truth to remember. For every monster in the world – murderer, rapist, whatever – there was a child who was abused. That doesn't excuse anything, but it's a good perspective to have in terms of how important it is to keep children safe. That was great... words kind of escape, actually, because it's something that happens on the set between two actors who are willing to be there in the moment. And then you try to comment on it later on, and words fail. But it's basically looking at a guy who understands me. It's saying, "We are totally screwed and you get it. I didn't expect that, because I didn't want to be you." Spike looks at Angel usually and all he can remember is all the evil that Angel did and can't really accept that *that* is ever going to be redeemed. It's like looking at Hitler and trying to make him redeemable. Come on! But what that means is that Spike isn't redeemable either, and so that's why Spike and Angel have that animosity for each other. At that moment, that kind

> "IF A PROJECT WAS OFFERED TO ME THAT WAS COOL AND HAD SPIKE IN IT, I WOULD LOVE TO DO IT. IT'S A FABULOUS CHARACTER, BUT AT THE SAME TIME, IT SEEMS TO BE OVER SO IT'S A GOOD TIME TO MOVE ON."

of dropped and we just kind of looked at each other and found that there was no need for animosity; that we were kind of in the same boat after a while.

WITH *ANGEL* COMING TO A CLOSE, AND WITH HAVING LOST *BUFFY*, DO YOU THINK THAT THIS IS THE END OF AN ERA FOR TELEVISION?
I'm hesitant to compare *Buffy the Vampire Slayer* to *Star Wars*, but I remember when *Star Wars* came out – I was a freshman in high school – and it absolutely raised the ante on the genre. There weren't really any good sci-fi pictures out there; there wasn't a real, incredible push that we expected out of the genre until *Star Wars*. I think Joss has done the same – certainly for vampires, if not for all of fantasy – he's upped the ante for what's possible in the genre. I think that people that approach the genre are going to have to be mindful of that or be behind the times. Joss used vampires to talk about human beings, so his vampires are so multi-dimensional because they're actually going through things that resonate with humans. The way we played vampires before was something very other-worldly that is scary and outside of us, and can really only go so far. That kind of formula can still work, but I think Anne Rice furthered it by really examining how they may be feeling about their situation and who they might be besides the pale face in the darkness, and Joss didn't take his cue from Anne Rice, but he did the same kind of thing. He explored them as people; what would it be like to live that long and what would it do to the psyche to kill that many people? This really plays out mostly with the souled vampires, because in Joss' realm, vampires, originally anyway, were just meant to be demonic. On both shows we switched styles so often that there's comedy, melo-drama, farce, realism, sometimes even naturalism, some stuff is

operatic – you can make fun of that and call it comedy, but what it is, actually, is something more in tune with the Shakespearean view of how you do storytelling, which works on all the levels. So, yes, I think it's the end of him taking his whack at the genre and I don't know if he'll return to it. He may – it's fertile ground. Let's face it, vampires rock! Anything you can say becomes cooler if a vampire's involved. A guy's mowing his lawn – he's a vampire. Guy walks into a liquor station and holds it up, the teller is a vampire. That twist just works.

SO YOU'RE TRULY READY TO MOVE ON AT THIS STAGE.
Whatever happens, I'll be proud of this my whole life. I told Sarah Michelle Gellar long ago, "We can get $10 million paychecks and be part of huge movies, but I don't know if we're ever going to touch a nerve like this again." I don't think any of us will ever have

an opportunity to play what we've played on these shows. I've said to Joss, "You know, this may be the best role I've ever had. I think this is better than the role of Macbeth." He blew that off, but I said, "Give me a second. Shakespeare is a great writer, but he only had three hours and he could only say so much in that time. You've had six years and you've used them really, really well."

THE ONE POSITIVE IS THAT YOU GUYS ARE GOING OUT ON TOP, CREATIVELY.
That's the one silver lining in all this, we're leaving them wanting more. They're picketing! What's beautiful is that they know it won't make a difference, but they want to express themselves and their love for the show. I think that that's just beautiful.

JAMES MARSTERS, THANK YOU VERY MUCH.

SPIKE TIMELINE

BY K. STODDARD HAYES

It's been more than 100 years of murder (hundreds, including two slayers!), madness (prusilla), and mayhem (pretty much everything else), so here's a handy chronological guide to ...

THE LIFE AND TIMES OF WILLIAM THE BLOODY

1880

Seeking a companion of her own, Drusilla sires a young English poet named William. William sires his beloved mom, and dusts her when she rejects his filial affection. Drusilla introduces him to her sire, Angelus, who, it transpires, is also her sometime lover. (*Buffy*: "Fool for Love", "Lies My Parents Told Me", *Angel*: "Destiny")

1890

While in China with Drusilla, Darla and Angelus, during the Boxer Rebellion, Spike kills his first Slayer, a Chinese girl. (*Buffy*: "Fool for Love"; *Angel:* "Darla")

1943

Spike is captured by Nazis and put aboard a submarine with other vamps as part of their plan to create an army of vampires. He and the other vamps escape and feed off most of the crew. Eventually, Angel (recruited by a secret branch of the government) puts Spike topside within sight of shore. (*Angel*: "Why We Fight")

1977

Spike kills his second Slayer, an African American woman named Nikki. He takes her black leather coat as a trophy. (*Buffy*: "Fool for Love")

1997

Spike arrives in Sunnydale with an enfeebled Drusilla, and demonstrates that he's the guy in charge, by dusting the Master's heir apparent. (*Buffy*: "School Hard")

Spike tries to use Angel's blood to heal Drusilla. In a battle with two Slayers, Drusilla is healed but Spike is crippled. (*Buffy*: "What's My Line")

1998

Angelus allies with Spike and Drusilla to take out the Slayer. Spike, jealous of Angelus' relationship with Drusilla, betrays Angelus and makes a deal with the Slayer so that he and Dru can escape from Sunnydale. (*Buffy*: "Innocence", etc. through to "Becoming")

1999

Dumped by Drusilla for his betrayal and his obsession with Buffy, Spike returns to Sunnydale to obtain a love spell from Willow, and messes up the lovelives of four of the Scoobies. (*Buffy*: "Lover's Walk")

2000-01

Spike returns to Sunnydale, hooks up with Harmony, and pursues the Ring of Amarra from Buffy's hands to Angel's in Los Angeles. (*Buffy*: "The Harsh Light of Day"; *Angel*: "In the Dark") Spike is captured by the Initiative, who put a chip in his head that prevents him from harming anything human. (*Buffy*: "The Initiative") He seeks protection from the Scooby Gang, and spends the next year or so making deals with anyone or anything to try to get rid of the chip.

Spike falls in love with Buffy, and woos her by trying to help fight Glory, exposing Riley's liaisons with vamps and offering to kill Drusilla for her. When she spurns him, he consoles himself by ordering Warren to make him a Buffybot.

Spike becomes a Scooby when he lets Glory half-kill him, rather than betray Dawn. (*Buffy:* "Intervention")

When Buffy is raised from the dead, Spike becomes her only confidant, and, for a little while, her lover.

2002

Buffy dumps Spike, and after attacking her, he goes on a quest to make himself worthy of her, by regaining his soul. ("Seeing Red")

Spike returns to Sunnydale with his soul, but without his marbles, and The First turns him into a secret weapon in its evil scheme.

Deciding that Spike is too dangerous to have around, Giles and Principal Wood, the son of the Slayer Nikki, plot to murder him behind Buffy's back. Spike comes to terms with the death of his mom, and breaks free of The First's control. (*Buffy*: "Lies My Parents Told Me")

2003

Using an amulet provided by Angel, Spike sacrifices himself in a blaze of glory to destroy The First's army of Ubervamps. (*Buffy*: "Chosen")

Spike's ghost shows up at Wolfram & Hart, and drives Angel nuts. (*Angel*: "Conviction")

Thanks to Lindsey McDonald, Spike becomes corporeal again. As part of a scheme against Angel and the Senior Partners, Lindsey sets up Spike as Angel's rival for the heroic role of vampire with a soul in the Shanshu prophecy. (*Angel*: "Destiny", "Soul Purpose")

2004

Spike has a run-in with a deranged Slayer, who forces him to look at his past crimes. (*Angel*: "Damage")

When Cordelia's return breaks up Lindsey's scheme, Spike loses his mission as solitary helper of the helpless, and returns to Wolfram & Hart. (*Angel*: "You're Welcome")

When Angel receives word that Buffy is living in Italy, and is in danger, him and Spike set off to rescue the woman they love from their old adversary, The Immortal, and come to a compromise about their feelings for The Slayer. (*Angel*: "The Girl in Question")

In the final showdown against The Senior Partners, Spike supports Angel, and the two vamps are left fighting the good fight side by side, their future looking bleak. ✦

Prophecy Boys

CONFUSED BY THE MINOR DETAILS OF THE SHANSHU PROPHECY IN *ANGEL*? WELL WORRY NO LONGER! *ANGEL MAGAZINE* INVESTIGATES THE ESSENTIAL SHANSHU FACTS!

When a Mohra demon's blood reverses his death, Angel becomes human again for one day. That episode, "I Will Remember You", shows us how much being human means to him: to feel his heart beat, to walk in sunlight, to enjoy the taste of food, and to share a perfect day with Buffy.

But the price of this happiness seems too high. The Oracles tell him that as a human, he can no longer serve the Powers That Be in the battle against the darkness, and he quickly learns that without his vampire strength and near-invulnerability, he's useless as a warrior. He gets his butt whipped by the Mohra demon, and has to watch Buffy risk her own life to protect him. Angel isn't ready to stop being a champion, and he certainly isn't ready to see Buffy die fighting alone. He gives up his happiness and persuades the Oracles to make him a vampire again.

Only a few months after this staggering, and apparently irreversible sacrifice, Angel steals an ancient scroll from Wolfram & Hart: the scroll of the Prophecies of Aberjian. Suddenly, the loss of Angel's humanity

By X

Stoddard Hayes

doesn't sound so irreversible. Wesley discovers a prophecy about "a vampire with a soul" who will "shanshu" if he survives "the coming darkness, the apocalyptic battles, a few plagues, and... several... fiends." Shanshu means "to die", but it doesn't mean the vampire will be killed. As Wesley explains, "A thing that's not alive never dies. It's saying that you get to live until you die... It's saying that you become human." He reads, "The vampire with a soul, once he fulfills his destiny, will shanshu, become human. It's his reward." ("To Shanshu in L.A.")

Angel and his friends are captivated by the hope that he might become human – which would very nicely wrap up the pesky problem of the gypsy curse, and finally allow him to enjoy some true happiness. He'd be free forever of the hunger for human blood that drives all vampires, and more important, free from the fear that Angelus might get loose again. In fact, Angel becoming human would finish Angelus for good: no vampire, no Angelus.

Too bad, though, that Angel's enemies aren't so interested in the human part of the prophecy. For most baddies, especially Wolfram & Hart, the central clause of the Shanshu prophecy is the one that states that the vampire with a soul will play a key role in some major apocalypse – though the prophecy doesn't state which side Angel will be on. In "Blood Money", Wolfram & Hart senior Nathan Reed makes it painfully clear to Lindsey and Lilah that Angel is far more important to the firm than they are, just because of that prophecy. The firm's belief

in Angel's importance leads to all kinds of trouble for Angel and his friends, especially the revival of Darla.

And the goddess who will be known as Jasmine takes great trouble to draw Angelus out into the world, as The Beast explains, shortly before Angelus skewers him with a dagger made of his own horn. Evil Cordelia/Jasmine has big plans for Angelus, partly because he's such a great party guy when it comes to causing darkness and mayhem. More importantly, as long as Angelus is around, Angel can't be there to meddle in any apocalypse of her making. Angel's defeat of Jasmine may or may not be the main Apocalypse referred to in the prophecy, but his friends do consider this a

Angel vs. Spike

Point by point, which of the boys really deserves to be the Shanshu vampire?

PLAYING A ROLE IN A MAJOR APOCALYPSE: Angelus killed The Beast, and Angel broke Jasmine's spell. He survived both these apocalypses. Spike used the amulet to destroy the armies of The First Evil and the Los Angeles Hellmouth, and sacrificed his own life.

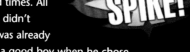

GETTING BACK YOUR SOUL: Angel's soul was restored by a curse the first time, by Willow's spell the second and third times. All three times, Angelus didn't want it back. Spike was already on his way to being a good boy when he chose to undergo a trial to win back his soul.

FAVOR OF THE POWERS THAT BE: The Powers sent Angel to help Buffy, then sent Doyle and the visions to help Angel in his fight. So far as we know, the Powers have never actually spoken to Spike.

FAVOR OF THE REAL POWERS THAT BE, TEAM WHEDON: No matter how much we love Blondie-bear, it's still Angel's show. ❧

Result: A tie!

{ "THERE IS A DESIGN, ANGEL, HIDDEN IN THE CHAOS AS IT MAY BE. BUT IT'S THERE. AND YOU HAVE YOUR PLACE IN IT..." WESLEY, "BLIND DATE" }

and peanut butter to look forward to). It means redemption. Angel has told Faith in "Orpheus" that he and she will never finish "doing their time," that the only way they can atone for their crimes is to fight the good fight for the rest of their lives. Yet somewhere in his deepest heart, Angel believes that if he can earn the reward of the prophecy, if he can earn the blessing of the Powers That Be, then perhaps he will have truly atoned for Angelus, and can finally be at peace.

DIVINE INTERVENTION

It takes divine intervention to straighten out this dueling Shanshu boys mess. In "You're Welcome", Cordelia wakes from her coma and calls the whole team back to their senses by reminding them what they're fighting for, and who they're sup- posed to be fighting: not each other, not legal battles for the clients of Wolfram & Hart, but Wolfram & Hart themselves. While she helps them expose Lindsey's plot to destroy Angel, and defeat Lindsey himself, that isn't her main purpose in get- ting this last holiday from the Powers. She's come to remind Angel that he is the true Champion, and that he is as much worth saving as everyone he fights for.

With Cordelia's last farewell, Spike renounces all claim to have a "destiny" and the Shanshu prophecy settles back on Angel's shoulders, where it seemed to begin. End of story? No, unhappily, it's not. The Senior Partners have another card to play, in trying to move Angel over to the wrong side of the field. When Angel infiltrates The Circle of the Black Thorn in "Not Fade Away", they bring him one final test to prove his loyalty to them and to the Senior Partners. They demand that he sign away – in his own blood – all claims to the Shanshu prophecy, and the hope of regaining his humanity.

Angel signs, of course. Oh,

strong indication that Angel is indeed the vampire in question.

SPIKE v ANGEL!

In Season Five, the Shanshu prophecy becomes a center-piece of the story arc. No doubt the Senior Partners had the prophecy in mind when they made their deal with Angel; getting him to work for them is the perfect way to control what role he might play in any apocalypse. However, the Senior Partners have a surprise or two coming themselves. When Lindsey secretly restores Spike to a corporeal state, Los Angeles suddenly has two vampire champions with souls. So which vampire gets to be, in Spike's words, "a real boy?"

Lindsey makes sure that Team Angel and the Senior Partners mistake Spike's resurrection for a cosmic problem. He uses some big-time magic to cause trouble at the Los Angeles office (well, "trouble" is a tiny understatement for a spell that makes most of the staff weep blood and go off in homicidal rages). Then his little sweet- heart, Eve, tells the team that the existence of two ensouled vampire champions is unraveling the fabric of reality. She makes it sound pretty convincing, too, explaining that Spike getting his soul back a year ago didn't cause a problem, because

Spike wasn't a true-blue champion until he sacrificed his life in the destruction of the Hellmouth (*Buffy*: "Chosen"). So now, Eve explains, the universe isn't big enough for both champions. Staff scholar Sirk, who's secretly in Lindsey's employ, tells them they'll have to decide who's the real champion, by racing to be the first to drink from a mystical cup, out in Death Valley (which, by the way, is in California, not Nevada as Sirk said. That should have tipped off Angel and the gang that Sirk was leading them up the Shanshu path!)

Lindsey may have hoped that Spike and Angel would kill each other over the cup. They don't, but even though the cup proves to be a fraud, filled with nothing more mystical than Mountain Dew, Angel is devastated that Spike got to it first. Spike has never before beaten him in a one-on- one fight. He tells Gunn that Spike just "wanted it more." And he wonders for the first time, "What if it means that I'm not the one?"

In "Soul Purpose", Angel is tormented by nightmares about being replaced by Spike, about being soulless and worthless. These nightmares reveal how important the Shanshu prophecy has become for him, now that its promise is slipping away. It means far, far more than just the hope of being human again (even with good love and the mad combination of chocolate c'mon, were you expecting him to weasel out of it? He's still the same guy who gave up humanity the first time he got it, because he wasn't ready to give up the fight. To him, this situation is no different. He has to keep fighting the dark, even if it means giving up all hope of that reward. And after all, it doesn't seem that big a loss to him at that moment, because, as he tells Spike, he's quite sure that he and his friends won't survive this battle anyway (which suits Spike fine, where the prophecy is concerned: "So long as it's not you," he snipes).

So Angel signs away his claim to the prophecy, and strides out into yet another apocalypse, swinging his sword and planning to slay a dragon. And that's the end of the Shanshu prophecy.

Or is it? For nearly five years, we've seen every major power from the Senior Partners on down, treat the Shanshu prophecy as incontrovertible truth, as something that will inevitably come to pass, one way or another. And it's still waiting to be fulfilled. So we have to ask, can the Circle's nasty bargain, even sealed with a champion's signature in blood (given, we point out, in a true champion spirit of sacrifice), really have the power to unwrite a major ancient prophecy? We don't think so. And maybe someday we'll find out.

The Shanshu Episodes

"Blind Date": Angel steals the scroll of the Prophecies of Aberjian from Wolfram & Hart, and Wesley reveals that the Prophecies include a section on the "vampire with a soul."

"To Shanshu in L.A.": Wesley determines that the passage which says the vampire with a soul will "shanshu" doesn't mean that vampire Angel will be killed. It means that his reward for fulfilling his destiny is to become human again.

"Blood Money": Lindsey and Lilah learn from their boss, that the prophecy says Angel will play a key role in some apocalypse, though it's not clear whether for good or evil.

"Reprise": Holland Manners, though dead, discusses the prophecy with Angel.

"Salvage": The Beast tells Angelus that the Rain of Fire, the blotting out of the sun, and stealing Angelus' soul were all done by his Master to bring forth and keep Angelus.

"Peace Out": Angel breaks Jasmine's spell, ends her reign, and possibly fulfills the prophecy's apocalypse clause.

"Hell Bound": Fred tells Spike about the Shanshu prophecy.

"Destiny": Lindsey and Eve trick Team Angel into thinking the prophecy might apply to Spike instead of Angel.

"Soul Purpose": Angel suffers from thinking he's not the Shanshu vampire, while Spike goes all Champion of Good with Lindsey posing as Doyle.

"You're Welcome": Cordelia helps Team Angel discover that Lindsey set up the rivalry between Spike and Angel. Angel gets his Shanshu mojo back, while Spike goes on a bender.

"Not Fade Away": To gain the trust of The Circle of the Black Thorn, Angel signs away his claim to the Shanshu prophecy and the hope of becoming a "real boy".

SEASON THREE'S "LULLABY" FINALLY SAW THE DEATH OF DARLA, AND AN END TO THE TEMPESTUOUS RELATIONSHIP SHE SHARED WITH ANGEL. K. STODDARD HAYES REFLECTS ON THEIR STORMY TIME TOGETHER.

Marriage Made in Hell

Angel, Darla and Three Centuries of Horror

`alway, Ireland, 1753: a drunken, womanizing youth named Liam quarrels yet again with his father, who throws him out of the house. Hating himself and his father, young Liam goes out to wallow in his vices, and meets a beautiful, seductive woman who promises to show him her world. Instead, she murders his humanity and becomes his vampire sire.

Welcome to love, Darla-style. It's her pleasure to destroy everything good, and to bring out the worst in her lover. After making Liam a vampire, she induces him to murder his entire family. Then, just as he's rejoicing in the satisfaction of killing

his father, she reveals that he has now destroyed any hope of winning his father's approval. It's her way of making sure that the rage and pain of Liam's relationship with his father will keep burning, and fuel the hatred that will make him into Angelus, the most vicious vampire ever known.

Left alone, Angelus might have been just an ordinary vampire, feeding and terrorizing in a (relatively) modest way. It's Darla who eggs him on to the greatest acts of destruction and horror. And it's Darla's actions that lead to the most horrendous consequences in Angel's life. She's his partner in the sadistic murder of Holtz's wife and children, a crime whose consequences will follow him right to the present day. It's Darla who brings Drusilla to

Angelus' notice, so that he drives the young clairvoyant mad before turning her into a vampire. Darla makes him a 'gift' of an innocent Gypsy girl to torment and terrorize.

This gift leads to the Gypsies' curse – the return of Angel's soul, which brings him decades of suffering and remorse, along with the ever-present fear of turning back into the demon Angelus.

With all the terrible consequences Darla's influence has had for Angel, it's ironic that she has done all this because she is obsessed with "her boy." He is the great love of her life – if love is the right word. She thinks that giving him the eternal life of the vampire is a great favor. The Gypsy curse may be the greatest disaster that has befallen her, because it separates her from Angelus. She rages at the Gypsies,

"You took him from me, you stole him away... What you have done will make him suffer for an eternity. Remove the filthy soul so that my boy might return to me."

When they meet again in Sunnydale, Darla still can't stand the idea that Angel is no longer "her boy," her Angelus. It's bad enough that he's interested in a mortal woman instead of her; but she's completely repulsed that his new squeeze is, of all people, the Slayer herself. Even the Master warns that her intense personal feelings will hinder her from doing the job of finishing the Slayer. And so it proves. Darla is not content with killing Angel or the Slayer in a straightforward way, by ambushing them with overwhelming numbers of vampires. She has to contrive a way that will cause "her boy" the deepest emotional hurt. She plans an attack on Buffy's mother, to make it

appear that Angel has attacked the Slayer's mother, so that the Slayer will attack Angel and one of them will be forced to kill the other.

Angel should hate Darla – she made him what he was; and made Angelus a far more terrifying monster than he might have been; it was her pleasure, always, to bring out the worst in him. The Master laments that Angelus was "the most vicious creature I ever knew. I miss him."

But when Darla comes to Angel's apartment in Sunnydale, we can see that he's still fascinated by her. Anyone with a clear head should be able to see right through Darla's seductive smirk, and her cooing about his true nature.

"You and I both know what you hunger for, what you need. You can only [hide] your real nature for so long. I can feel it brewing inside of you. I hope I'm around when it explodes."

When she steps up close to him, stroking his chest and smiling as she whispers at him, he doesn't move away. As much as he's afraid of what she offers, he's still under her spell.

ANGEL'S PAST: A Timeline

K. STODDARD HAYES PIECES TOGETHER THE VARIOUS ANGEL FLASHBACKS, TO PROVIDE A CHRONOLOGICAL LOOK AT THE LIVES OF ANGEL/ANGELUS AND DARLA.

1609, Virginia Colony. A prostitute dying of syphilis is visited by a 'priest', the Master, who brings her into his immortal demon flock and renames her 'Darla'. ("Darla")

1753, Ireland. Drunken, debauched no-good son Liam is thrown out of the house by his father, and seduced by the beautiful Darla. She turns him into a vampire and induces him to murder his entire family. ("The Prodigal")

1760, London. Darla introduces Angelus to her sire, the Master. Angelus mocks the Master his "bat nose" and the "r infested sewer" he lives in and lures Darla to leave v him in search of the good life. ("Darla")

fascination and look her in the face when he killed her, because when Darla is resurrected by Wolfram & Hart, Angel discovers just how much is still unresolved in this relationship.

For Darla, things haven't changed much at first. She's delighted with the chance to torment Angel, but what she really wants, as always, is to have "her boy" back. She's sure that all she has to do is get him to make love to her, so that he'll have a moment of perfect happiness, and lose his soul again. Before long, though, she begins to feel her mortality, and the pain of being human.

Angel believes that he understands Darla's pain, because, like him, she has regained her soul after being a demon for hundreds of years. When he saves her from Wolfram & Hart's assassins, he discovers how far apart they still remain. Angel wants to help Darla live through the pain, as he did. Darla, still newly human, doesn't want to live through the pain. Like Angel a hundred years ago, right after he regained his soul, Darla just wants to put things back the way they were. She wants Angel to make her a vampire again.

"For 100 years, you've not had a moment's peace because you will not accept what you are. That's all you have to do. Accept it. Kill! Feed! Live!",

she urges, revealing her true intentions. Yes, she wants to kill the Slayer, the enemy of her kind. But even more, she wants Angelus back. She's hoping that he'll be driven to kill the Slayer, and that will turn him back to a monster and her lover.

All Angel has to do is stake her – or at the very least, throw her out of his apartment and refuse to listen to her temptations. But Angel's never had a clear head where Darla is concerned. She was his lover and companion for

150 years. Not exactly a human notion of romantic bliss, as they terrorized Europe together, yet the emotional attachment is undeniable. Even after the Gypsy curse restores his soul, Angel tries to return to Darla. He follows her all the way to China, and tries to convince her he can be Angelus. Much as Darla wants to believe him, she isn't fooled for long. She notices that he smells of rat blood, and that he has only killed criminals, not the good and innocent people she despises. She is as repulsed and disgusted with his virtue as only bitter disappointment can be.

A hundred years later, Darla still has so strong a hold on Angel that he can't even face her when he stakes her to save Buffy. He comes at her from behind, before she can turn and speak to him. He does what he has to, to save Buffy's life. But it would certainly have been better for him, if he had found the strength to overcome his

---

1764, York, England. While vampire hunter Daniel Holtz is hunting Angelus and Darla, they return to his home, where they rape and murder his wife, murder his infant son, and turn his daughter into a vampire, whom Holtz is forced to kill. ("Quickening", "Lullaby")

1765, France. Pursued by Holtz, Darla and Angelus take refuge in a barn, where Darla betrays Angelus and takes their only horse so she can escape. ("The Trial")

1767, Marseilles, France. Angelus, Darla and their new companions, the vampire lovers James and Elizabeth, make another last minute escape from the vampire hunter Holtz. ("Heartthrob")

1771, Rome. Holtz and a rogue order of monks capture Angel and begin to torture him. Darla and some vamps rescue him, killing most of Holtz's allies, but leaving Holtz alive. ("Offspring")

1774, York, England. Holtz is transported out of his own time by the demon SahJhan, who intends to have Holtz destroy Angel and Darla before their son can be born. ("Quickening")

1860, London. Darla induces Angel to torment a young clairvoyant girl named Drusilla.

"I gave you eternal life. Now you can return the favor."

"Favor?" says Angel.

"Is that what you think it is?"

Angel tries to save Darla's human life by undergoing a trial; perhaps it's his heroism, or perhaps the voice of her own soul that persuades Darla to accept her mortality. Unfortunately, Drusilla takes the choice out of her hands, by raising her 'grandmother' back to vampire life. Darla's return to her vampire state throws Angel into the worst darkness he has known since he regained his soul. It's while hunting her that he leaves a party of Wolfram & Hart attorneys to die at the hands of the vamp women. And it's while hunting her that he fires his closest friends, and goes off on his own, refusing to accept comfort or counsel. And in his darkness, when Darla returns to him after he tries to kill her, he spends the night with her.

It's a night that, by Darla's reckoning,

should give Angel the perfect happiness that will turn him back into Angelus. Instead, it destroys all her assumptions about her relationship with Angel. When the night is over, he is still Angel, still the vampire with a soul. Darla is appalled to discover that she couldn't give him that moment of perfect happiness. He may be her true love, but she was never his.

Of course, that night has another fateful consequence. Months later, Darla returns to L.A., pregnant with Angel's child. Though she doesn't seem to have changed much at first, her return does demonstrate that Angel has changed in one important way. When Darla tries to bite Cordelia, Angel comes very close to killing her, face to face. He, at least, has finally gotten over his obsession with her.

Yet he has not ceased to care for her and hope for her redemption, and he

protects her and the unborn child. When the child's soul begins to stir in Darla, she begins to change. No longer eager to let it die or cut it from her body, she confesses to Angel that she feels a love for the child, and that love comes from the presence of the child's soul in her. But she knows that her love for the child will perish as soon as it leaves her body.

Ultimately, Darla stakes herself and dies, leaving a healthy human baby boy amid her ashes. She's saved her child, and probably ensured herself of whatever salvation a vampire can have. But the child will grow up as Holtz's foster son Stephen. And Holtz will raise his adopted son to hate his biological father above all things, because of what Angelus and Darla did to his family. In spite of her last wishes, Darla's legacy of bringing hell on earth to Angel continues... ✢

He drives her mad by torturing and murdering her family before her eyes, then he follows her to a convent and sires her into the life of the vampire. ("Dear Boy")

1880, London. Angel and Darla suggest that Drusilla find herself a playmate. She chooses a heartbroken, awful poet wannabe

named William, who will soon earn the nickname "Spike." ("Darla")

1898, Romania. Darla gives Angelus a gift: a young Gypsy girl, who happens to be the favorite of her clan. The Gypsies

curse Angelus with a soul. In revenge for taking "her boy" away from her, Darla and her family massacre the Gypsies. ("Five by Five")

1900, China. Angel catches up with Darla during the Boxer Rebellion, and tries to convince her to take him back. Doubting his ability to commit mayhem, she demands that he prove himself by feeding on a baby. Angel grabs the baby and escapes. ("Darla")

1952, Los Angeles. Having retired to the New World, Angel lives in seclusion in the Hyperion Hotel. When the hotel's other residents blame him for his recent murders, and lynch him, he leaves them to the mercy of the paranoia demon that possesses the hotel. ("Are You Now or Have You Ever Been...?") ✢

Angel's Happy Family

Where vampires are involved, is blood really thicker than water? k. Stoddard Hayes takes a look at Angel's (vampire) nearest and not-so-dearest.

Grandsire: The Master

Origin: Older than we can imagine.
Comeuppance: Killed by the Slayer, and his bones mashed to dust so he can't be raised again.

Sire: Darla

Human origin: Prostitute in early 17th century America, suffering terminal syphilis.
Vampire origin: Sired by the Master on her deathbed.
Comeuppance: Staked by Angel while trying to kill Buffy.

Angel / Angelus

Human origin: Liam, eldest son of an Irish-family.
Vampire origin: Sired by Darla, who induces him to murder his family and most of his neighbors.
Redemption: A Gypsy curse restores his soul, leaving him in eternal torment.
Vamp resurrection: After Angel experiences a moment of perfect happiness with Buffy, the curse makes him lose his soul and become the vicious Angelus again.
Comeuppance: Buffy runs Angelus through with a sword, and sends him to a hell dimension.
Second Redemption: Willow succeeds in restoring his soul just as he departs for the hell dimension; when he returns, he's Angel again.

Vampire Daughter: Drusilla

Human origin: A girl with powerful psychic abilities, who is driven mad by Angelus' torments.
Vampire origin: Sired by Angelus in a convent, just as she is preparing to take final vows.
Comeuppance: Burned by Angel after going on a rampage in LA; she survives and her whereabouts are unknown.

Human Son: Connor

Origin: The first ever child produced by two vampires. Grew up in a Hell Dimension, and returned to the present day a teenager.

Vampire Granddaughter: Darla

Human origin: Resurrected as a human by Wolfram & Hart as a tool to defeat Angel.
Vampire origin: Sired by Drusilla to save her "grandmother" from a very human death by syphilis.
Comeuppance: Seduces Angel in the hope of giving him the moment of "perfect happiness" that will restore Angelus to her. It doesn't, but she conceives a child.
Redemption: While in labor, stakes herself to bring the child safely into the world, and prevent herself from harming the child.

Vampire Grandson: William the Bloody (Spike)

Human origin: Sentimental and appallingly bad Romantic poet.
Vampire origin: Sired by Drusilla for some companionship.
Comeuppance: A chip installed by the Initiative prevents him from harming humans, and forces him to become one of the Scoobies.
Redemption? After enduring a series of trials to getting rid of the chip, Spike is returned to what he was – he gets his soul back. Being in love with Buffy might help, too.

IT'S AMAZING WHAT A LITTLE TRIP
TO A HELL DIMENSION CAN DO TO
YOU. JUST LOOK AT ANGEL'S SON,
CONNOR. HOLTZ TOOK HIM INTO
QUOR'TOTH AS A LITTLE BABY,
AND A FEW DAYS LATER
(OUR TIME) HE EMERGES AS A
BROODING TEENAGER! ACTOR
VINCENT KARTHEISER TALKS
US THROUGH CONNOR'S
TROUBLED TIME ON *ANGEL*.

BY PAUL SIMPSON

HELL B

ANGEL MAGAZINE: HOW DID YOU GET INVOLVED WITH *ANGEL*?

VINCENT KARTHEISER: I got involved with the show towards the end of 2001. I'd been doing features most of my career and I'd done a couple of guest stars on TV, but I wanted to get a little more routine in my life, so I decided I would go out and do some television. A couple of projects came to me before *Angel*, but I passed on them. I wasn't interested.

What really made me interested in *Angel* was the idea that as a show, it changed so much and all the characters could change so much. One week there could be a spell where you were acting completely opposite than every other episode you had done. It wasn't that cliched kind of 'show up, do your thing, go home' all the time. There was always a new twist. Every week I got a script, and I opened it up wondering what was going to happen not only with my character but on a broad scale. So I went in and met with Tim Minear, who's a wonderful man, and Joss Whedon. I did a read, then David Greenwalt brought me back, I met David Boreanaz and there we were.

DID YOU FOLLOW *BUFFY* OR *ANGEL* BEFORE YOU WERE CAST?

No. And I [didn't] even follow *Angel* [when I was] on it. I'm the type of person who really enjoys sports, and really enjoys the Discovery Channel and The Learning Channel – shows about going into the depths of the ocean. I do drama 15 hours a day. The last thing I do when I get home is flip on a dramatic show! Before I started on *Angel*, my agent sent me all the tapes for the show, so that's what gave me all these inner eyes into what I was getting myself into. After they showed me the pilot episode and a couple of other ones, I was sold.

WHAT DID YOU GET TOLD ABOUT CONNOR WHEN YOU STARTED?

When I came into the project it was for three episodes, with an option to pick me up for as many seasons as they liked, which at that point was five because that would make it concurrent with everyone else's contracts. They never really let me know that it was going to be a one-season thing. I felt that it was anyway. There were some things that had happened before I came on. When Connor was just a baby on the show, they said, 'The father will kill the son'. That was one of the things that Wesley found. So I always had that in the back of my head.

As the season went on, we never really got the opportunity to deal with the relationship problems between me and David. I never really got the opportunity to bond with any other characters. There were a couple of scenes which I thought were the start of something. I remember J. [August Richards, Gunn] and I did that scene where we're digging a grave and I looked over at J. and said, 'This is going to be the beginning of our bonding relationship'. Then the next episode we were back to being competitive enemies again. So I started to get an inkling for it about halfway through the season, because I was thinking, 'Where are they going to go? My character doesn't fit with *Angel* because we've never dealt with the issue', and no-one else really seemed to like the character of Connor too much.

CONNOR SEEMS TO SCARE THE HELL OUT OF THEM.

Yeah, and he's also afraid of them, He's not used to this world and he's really not one of them. While they have all these relationships with each other, he's very much away from that and very angry. He's not willing to open up to this kind of group happiness that everyone else is so inclined to be part of.

WHAT DID YOU MAKE OF THE LIFE THAT HE'D HAD AWAY WHEN HE WAS GROWING UP?
When I auditioned for this role, the script that they gave me said 'street kid'. It said nothing about being Angel's son, and said nothing about Quor'Toth. So about two weeks before I started filming they sent me the script and it said that he's a demon slayer from another dimension. For me, it was like, 'How do I do this?' So I turned off all the lights in my apartment, I got stark naked and I crawled around on my hands and knees killing imaginary demons. I showed up to work the first day, and my character was kind of bent over, and I had this real living-in-the-brush kind of 'failed being' attitude, and they said no to that right away. They cut that out! They were like, 'No, no, no; stand up straight, normal voice' – they wanted what I did in the audition, which was 'street kid'. They just wanted a regular character to come on. That halted my process where it had begun and I had to start over.

But what I make of Connor's past is that your past is what you know. If you're born in a third world country living in sewage, it's what you know. I think there were times when he was in Quor'Toth that maybe he thought there was something better out there, but I don't think he thought he could ever get there. Holtz would maybe tell him about it, but I don't think he would ever really believe it, or could ever really see it. I think he had fun in Quor'Toth. I think he enjoyed killing demons. And I think the only reason he ever came to this world was to please Holtz, and to do what he felt he was born to do.

EVERYTHING HE'S TOLD IS A LIE TO THE END. DID THAT BECOME DIFFICULT TO PLAY?
I guess the lie isn't so hard to play when you believe it. With Jasmine, if your character believes the lie, you just play it like you believe it. And with the other trust issues, that's not so much hard to play, as

it's hard sometimes to stomach. You'll do one thing in one episode and then the next episode someone else is writing and it will come at you from a completely different angle. You say, 'That's not congruent with what I just did last episode; I had trust issues with this person, and now I'm opening up to them'. There was a while there when me and Charisma were together where I was trying to kind of turn her against Angel. And I was definitely not for him. But then I still went to him and said, 'You should come talk to her'. I was kind of opening up and bringing him back into it, and showing the good side of Connor, but it also was a little bit hypocritical. From week to week I am different. From week to week I am a hypocrite. So you just have to play into that and that's what I did.

PRESUMABLY CHARISMA (CORDELIA) CARPENTER'S PREGNANCY MUST HAVE CHANGED THE WAY THINGS WERE GOING.
It did change the season a bit. I don't necessarily know where they were going to go with it, but I do know that whenever something like that happens, it's going to change things.

HOW MUCH OF A PRACTICAL CHANGE DID IT MAKE TO YOU ON SET?
Not a lot. There are much worse issues than people being pregnant, unfortunately, in this industry. I've worked with actors that have much bigger problems than that. You had to be sensitive about some things. I'm a smoker so I would have to go back to my trailer to smoke. We would try to work around [Charisma]. Sometimes we would shoot her out fast, but not a lot. Actually she had an abundance of energy for a working, pregnant lady who, right in the heart of her preg-

don't know what I brought to it. But I brought it!

DO YOU THINK CONNOR BROUGHT A SHARPER EDGE INTO THE SHOW?
Having Connor there allowed J. to change Gunn. I think with shows like this you constantly have to be surprising the audience. You constantly have to be bringing in new characters, new situations and new demographics, and a new energy to it. I'd like to think that all of us are different and all of us bring something. But I leave that to David [Greenwalt] and Joss to say what it is.

CONNOR IS NOT GOING TO BE A REGULAR CHARACTER IN SEASON FIVE. WOULD YOU LIKE TO COME BACK FROM TIME TO TIME?
Yes. It's a sensitive question, but I would love to come back. To tell you honestly, this is the best group of people I've ever worked with. I'm saying 'people' – as artists, they're very accomplished and as people their set was so pleasant and I had so much fun, I really made some good friends there. It was nice for me to have that stability in my life. I'm really going to miss that, and I'm really going to miss some of the opportunities that it gave me too, to stretch and to try some things. But I'm also looking forward to going on and doing some new stuff. I never really wanted to do five seasons, so one season I feel was nice. And hopefully they do want me back. Tim [Minear] spoke to me about bringing me back for a few episodes, and I would definitely do that.

WE DON'T KNOW HOW HE'LL END UP WITH HIS NEW FAMILY...
Yeah, hopefully we'll see that arc. That's the thing with *Angel*: I could presume

nancy, they put her in so much. I was so surprised. But it worked, and I think she did well with it. But to me it didn't change anything.

WHAT DO YOU THINK YOU BROUGHT TO THE SHOW AS AN ACTOR?
I have no idea what they saw in me. But I think as many people in this world, I feel that we generally think lower of ourselves than others do. Abraham Lincoln said, 'I would never be with a woman who would have me as her husband'. It's kind of that idea that you go

into these things and you do your thing, then you walk on and you say, 'Oh I'm terrible. Who would ever want to work with me?' I rely on others to see something in me. I try not to focus too much on myself, because I think that part of everyone's acting should be an ability to leave the body, an ability to forget your own insecurities. That all comes back when you're driving home and you go, 'Sh*t, I should have done that totally different! I just got an idea for that scene, and oh, I wish I'd done it.' But on the day, you honestly do your best. I

{ "I WOULD LOVE TO COME BACK [TO ANGEL]. THIS IS THE BEST GROUP OF PEOPLE I'VE EVER WORKED WITH. I HAD SO MUCH FUN, I REALLY MADE SOME GOOD FRIENDS THERE." }

everything I wanted, and chances are it's going to be totally different than that.

OF ALL YOUR EPISODES ON *ANGEL*, DO YOU HAVE ANY FAVORITE MOMENTS, SCENES, BOTH AS AN ACTOR AND ALSO AS THE CHARACTER?

When I first arrived, I loved every fight scene, some more than others, but it was so great to play a character that was truly badass. I've done fight scenes before on movies but it's always been 'punch, punch, fall down'. This is like choreographed fighting. All of that was amazing for me. I really enjoyed the scenes with David when we did confront the issue between Angel and Connor. That to me was the soul of this character. The name of the show is *Angel* so it all comes back to him. For Connor, everything stems from this place with

Angel and Holtz, and when we got the opportunity for him to let that out, I think he came out of his rough shell and showed a little bit of his sensitivity. He showed that he was hurt by his father and that he was hurt by Holtz. Those scenes I really enjoyed doing.

WHAT'S BEEN THE BIGGEST CHALLENGE YOU'VE FACED AS AN ACTOR IN YOUR CAREER?

Myself. I've been the biggest challenge. In life I feel that we tend to self-sabotage. I have to deal with some of my fear issues and I have to take some more risks. There are times that I've really gotten down on myself for things, and I've really started to believe terrible things about myself. I've let whoever's hiring me dictate my own feelings about myself and then let that fester and that's become an envious or an ill-placed energy. It's

ANGEL MAGAZINE: CONNOR WENT THROUGH SOME MAJOR EVENTS IN SEASON FOUR, AND VINCENT KARTHEISER PERFORMED IT ALL VERY WELL, WOULDN'T YOU SAY?

JOSS WHEDON: Yes. And [it's] great to see Connor happy for a change. The poor guy. He had every reason to be angry. He [only] got to smile like, once last season. He's the Dawn [Summers] of *Angel*.

[Connor] had a really, really bad childhood... But now he's having a really nice one, and eating nice meals with a family that loves him and who won't kidnap him and take him to Quor'toth.

IN EPISODE ONE, "CONVICTION," YOU'VE OPENED UP OLD WOUNDS ANGEL HAS OVER LOSING HIS OWN SON, CONNOR, THROUGH THE FATHER/SON STORYLINE OF THE EVIL FRIES AND HIS INNOCENT SON, MATTHEW.

We have to introduce a bunch of mythology to people who have never seen the show and I debated whether or not to throw that in since the idea was that he's changed history and, according to everybody else, nobody knows that he ever had a son so it doesn't really affect the episode. But I thought it would be nice to put it in because it makes what happens affect Angel on more than just an, 'I'm having an ethical dilemna!' sort of [level]. It punches him in the gut, which is what he needs. It's also a sense that we will see Connor again at some point...

BY TRACY BELLOMO

{ "WHEN I FIRST ARRIVED, I LOVED EVERY FIGHT SCENE. IT WAS SO GREAT TO PLAY A CHARACTER THAT WAS TRULY BADASS. I REALLY ENJOYED THE SCENES WITH DAVID." }

CASTING
KARTHEISER

ANGEL MAGAZINE: WHAT DO YOU LOOK FOR IN A SCRIPT OR PROJECT?
VINCENT KARTHEISER: Well, it's changed. When I was young – 16, 17 years old – it was all about character for me. I really wanted to do things that I felt I could believe, and that I felt had an arc – a beginning, a middle and an end. The character grew. I always grow from those experiences. Whenever a character grows then I feel like I grow in a sense. And although I leave it behind I feel parts of that always stay with you.

As I'm getting older, character still plays a very vital role in everything, but now I'm also looking to work with accomplished directors, to work with people who won't settle for second best. I want to work with people who when I do something that isn't fitting or when I'm doing something that's not authentic really push me to go further. Not insult me and say, 'Do it better', but really work with me to go further. It's a collaborative thing. Whenever you show up on a set you go to the director and say, 'Hey, I know you're directing the scene, but I have an idea'. Sometimes he'll say, 'That doesn't work', sometimes he'll say it does. It's the same with actors. I have worked with some people, as we all have, who don't bring anything and leave it all in your hands. I'm not the kind of actor who's going to come onto a set and feel over-secure about what I'm doing. I want to be pushed and I want to be stretched. 🦇

{ "WHAT REALLY MADE ME INTERESTED IN ANGEL WAS THE IDEA THAT AS A SHOW, IT CHANGED SO MUCH AND ALL THE CHARACTERS COULD CHANGE SO MUCH. THERE WAS ALWAYS A NEW TWIST." }

only made me stagnant and pushed me backward. As an actor the challenges are numerous when it comes to character development. It's all in the details. Sometimes you get situations where the details are very obvious. You can look at a character and you go, 'Okay, I get it, this guy's a punk, he lives on the street, here are the details. I want this kind of shirt, I want this kind of wallet, I want him to ride this kind of bike'. Sometimes you read a script and it tells you nothing. It says 'James, 22' and the dialogue could be written for anyone. For me, a big challenge is taking that, reading the script over and over and finding what details are going to help me find a voice for this character.

WHAT DO YOU THINK YOU'RE GOING TO TAKE AWAY FROM

ANGEL TO THE NEXT ROLES YOU PLAY?

As an actor I think I leave the character behind. I did have some opportunities to stretch. There were parts of the season I didn't have opportunities to stretch, that it felt like I was doing the same scene over and over. Towards the end of the season I was really happy about the chances I was getting. I was really happy about the opportunities in the last episode. The scenes went really well and I was really glad. But generally what I take from *Angel* is what I take from every job, in a sense. Every little bit of information that you pick up every time you're on a set helps you and pushes you forward. But character-wise, I leave it behind. You do your thing and then you have to leave it, whether you are happy or not with it, or whether it was good enough. You're only as good as

the next thing you're doing. I don't want to stay back there, you know; I've got to keep moving ahead.

VINCENT KARTHEISER, THANK YOU VERY MUCH! 🦇

– THANKS TO SEAN HARRY OF STARFURY.

VINCENT KARTHEISER SELECTED CREDITS

– FILM –

Untamed Heart (1993) – Orphan boy
Little Big League (1994) – James
Heaven Sent (1994) – Eddie Chandler
The Indian in the Cupboard (1995) – Gillon
Alaska (1996) – Sean Barnes
Masterminds (1997) – Oswald 'Ozzie' Paxton
Strike! (1998) – Snake
Another Day in Paradise (1998) – Bobbie
Crime and Punishment in Suburbia (2000) – Vincent
Preston Tylk (2000) – Dillon
Luckytown (2000) – Colonel
Ricky 6 (2000) – Ricky Cowen
The Unsaid (2001) – Thomas Caffey
Falling Off the Verge (2003) – Deeter
Dandelion (2003) – Mason Mullich

– TV –

E.R. (1994) – Jesse Keenan
Angel (2001-2003) – Connor

ANGEL

ANGEL'S SCHOOL
OF
BUSINESS
MANAGEMENT

DIPLOMA of
BUSINESS
STUDIES

№   0666

"LETS GO TO
WORK"

BY KATE ANDERSON

ASIDE FROM BEING A CRIME-FIGHTING CREATURE OF THE NIGHT, ANGEL HAS ALSO PROVED TO HAVE A RATHER GOOD HEAD FOR BUSINESS ON THOSE HUNKY SHOULDERS. FROM SETTING UP A PRIVATE INVESTIGATIONS AGENCY, TO RUNNING A HOTEL (OF SORTS) AND HEADING A TOP LAW FIRM, THE BROODING ONE HAS BUILT UP A RATHER IMPRESSIVE RESUME OF SUCCESSFUL VENTURES. INSPIRED BY ANGEL'S ENTREPRENEURIAL SKILLS, WE PRESENT ANGEL'S TOP TIPS FOR RUNNING A SUCCESSFUL BUSINESS.

Think about profits. It's a business boys, not a batcave.
(HAMILTON)

Tip Number 1 – It's All About Team Work

When it comes to running any successful business, team work can be the difference between success and failure. So, it's essential to pick the best, most suitable employee(s) for the job(s). Variety is the spice of life, and you need talented individuals that, whilst bringing their own skills and personalities to the job, can also compliment one another and bring out the best in their colleagues. Usually, potential candidates can be broken down into various categories. For example, there's the shy but adorable brain; the sassy, sarcastic cutie who always thinks they know what's best; the lovable, roguish joker; the streetwise smart ass; the bookworm with an encyclopaedic knowledge; and the born entertainer. Above all, it's important to remember that good working relations between colleagues means happy employees, and happy employees means a happy boss. And besides, you're going to be working day in, day out with these people. So, you wouldn't want them to be boring, now, would you?!

Tip Number 2 – Image is Everything

Whatever line of business you're in, you need to look the part. For example, gone are the days when you need to look like Magnum to be a P.I.! Forget the dodgy tash and garish Hawaiian shirts, to play detective you need to be able to blend into the background and not stick out like a sore thumb. Although it's a different rule when it comes to your car – in fact, the flashier and sportier the better! Of course, being a creature of the night means that lurking in dark alleyways comes naturally. Perhaps that's why vamps seem to favor black. Besides, haven't you heard, black is the new, er... black – not to mention the essence of cool. On the other hand, if you're heading up a prestigious law firm, money shouldn't be an object, so you should be able to afford the smartest of designer business suits. Just because your clients may be the scum of the universe, it doesn't mean you can't look respectable!

Tip Number 3 – Be Prepared to Give Up Your Social Life

Forget any idea you might have about having any kind of a social life. Drinks with the lads; watching sports; salsa dancing... whatever you enjoy doing on your days off, forget it! Work has to come first, and the more you put into your business, the more you'll get out of it. So, if you're thinking about working for yourself, it makes sense to do something you love; something you're going to feel passionate about. Oh, and forget having any kind of relationship – you won't have the time or the energy! In fact, don't be surprised if you start to feel like you're married to the job! Running a detective agency or an evil law firm, for example, is never going to be a nine to five job. And you can forget about weekends off. If you have aspirations of helping the helpless and saving the world, expect to be on call 24/7, because evil doesn't clock in and clock off. Just ask Batman!

Tip Number 4 – Know Your Market

In other words, you have to know what it is you're selling – and more importantly, whom you're selling it to. Of course, it helps if your product or service has longevity. With the way the world is, there will always be a market for a champion to fight for humanity in the dark and seedy underside of cities like Los Angeles. Not to mention lawyers to represent those that have committed acts of crime, or detectives to trail cheating spouses and trace missing loved ones. The good versus evil business is manic. But, as Wolfram & Hart proved, it can also be a very prosperous one, too. Remember – it's all about supply and demand. So, if you can provide the evil, and the champion to tirelessly fight it, everyone's a winner!

Why do people keep putting me in charge of things!
(WESLEY)

OFFICE ANGEL?

HE'S BEEN A P.I. AND RUN A SUCCESSFUL (ALBEIT EVIL) LAW FIRM. BUT WHAT ELSE COULD ANGEL PERHAPS TURN HIS HAND TO? WE ANALYZE A VARIETY OF POSSIBLE CAREERS ANGEL MIGHT CONSIDER, SHOULD HE EVER FIND HIMSELF UNEMPLOYED – OR FED UP OF FIGHTING THE GOOD FIGHT. OH, AND LET'S NOT FORGET THE ONES HE SHOULD DEFINITELY AVOID – AT ALL COSTS!

Pub landlord – Well, he is Irish, and the Irish, as we all know, are well-known for their hospitality! Hmm, we wonder if Angel could do the hippy hippy shake? If he needs some pointers, he could always ask Xander.

Estate agent – Slick, moody, charming... sounds like your average estate agent! And Angel sure does cut a fine figure in a business suit!

Pop star – While there's no doubt Angel's got the looks to cut it as a pop star (although he might be a tad too old for a boy band!), he does however lack one essential ingredient – a good singing voice! Although that never stopped the Spice Girls!

Tip Number 5 – Have Plenty of Good Contacts

As that old saying goes, it's not what you know, but who you know. Well, something like that! But whatever you're doing to earn a crust and pay those bills, it helps to have plenty of friends – and particularly friends in high places. And they don't come much higher than the likes of The Oracles and The Powers That Be. In other words, a bulging contacts book should ensure that those pennies keep rolling in. And if you can employ the services of a wise-cracking Irishman or sassy lass with powerful visions, you'll be laughing all the way to the bank.

Tip Number 6 – Never Mix Business With Pleasure

Mixing business and pleasure in the work place is always going to be risky. It can cause friction on the highest scale. If it's not the awkward glances in the canteen, it's the constant whispers and jealous glances between colleagues. And heaven forbid if you have an argument and refuse to speak to one another, never mind work together!

Yes, office relationships will always be dicey territory. In fact, walking bare foot over hot stones might be a preferable option to a failed office romance (or a magic-induced clinch – how embarrassing!).

Tip Number 7 – Be Prepared to Make Sacrifices

As an old wise man once said, no reward comes without sacrifice. Well, he probably didn't but it sounds good, all the same! Yes, you name it, you might have to sacrifice it: personal life, relationships, friends, family, etc.

Unfortunately, sometimes success comes with a very high price. And if you're running an evil law firm, where you have to face off against all sorts of unsavory characters – not to mention deal with a potential apocalypse – that could even mean making the most ultimate of all sacrifices. Kind of makes giving up chocolate seem like a walk in the park.

Construction worker – We bet Angel would look heavenly in a pair of grubby overalls. He's got the perfect physique for hard labor; just watching him flex those muscles as he, er… constructs, would be a sight for sore eyes. Particularly during the hot summer months – so he'd have to take his shirt off! However, the whole 'outdoors' thing could be an issue…

Dentist – Ever seen a vampire with bad teeth? Exactly!

Car salesman – Honest, reliable, trustworthy, with excellent body work – and no, we're not talking about the car! Okay, so Angel may not look like your average car salesman, but we reckon buying a used motor from this man would be a safe bet. (And he's an expert on cars, you know!)

Celebrity bodyguard – Angel's got all the right moves and he certainly knows how to handle himself in a fight. Plus, he hates the limelight, so there's no chance of him getting more attention than his celebrity clients. And a good-looking bodyguard is a celebrity essential.

Bike courier – Angel was born to wear black leather. Although just make sure his crash helmet isn't shocking pink!

"My company rocks." (LILAH)

Tip Number 8 – Always Be One Step Ahead Of The Competition

It's a dog eat dog world out there. If you want to be the best of the best, then you're going to have to tread on a fair few toes to get there. To be at the top of your game, you always need to be one step ahead of the competition. And if that means eliminating your rivals, so be it!

Tip Number 9 – The Customer is Always Right

Especially if they can liquefy your insides with just one look, turn you into a fuzzy puppet (it happens!) or happen to have all the minions of Hell and a fire-breathing dragon at their disposal... 'Nuff said!

"A lone wolf such as myself never works with anyone. I'm merely allowing Angel to assist me."

(WESLEY)

Counselor – He may be a good listener, but let's face it, Angel's not exactly known for his communication skills. However, having lived a very long and full life, he should have a wealth of experience to offer good advice. Particularly when it comes to forbidden love, split personalities and feeling like an outsider.

History teacher – Angel would make the perfect history teacher. Considering he was born way back in the 18th Century, he's going to have first hand experience of many of the most historic moments in history.

Lifeguard – He might look hunky in a pair of red swimming trunks, but the sun is a big no-no for vampires. No amount of sun block in the world would prevent Angel from burning up – quite literally. Although Angel probably doesn't like getting his hair wet anyway.

Doctor – Well, for starters, he's not squeamish when it comes to blood. And we're sure he'd look sexy in a white coat – he'd certainly give George Clooney a run for his money in the dashing doctor stakes! And no doubt he'd have a bedside manner to die for. Although not literally, we hope!

NOT ON
ACTIVE DU

ROHM

— FROM —

R✦HM

[B Y   A B B I E   B E R N S T E I N]

KATE LOCKLEY MAY HAVE ONLY STARRED IN 15 EPISODES OF *ANGEL*, BUT SHE LEFT A LASTING IMPRESSION ON *ANGEL* FANS. WE CAUGHT UP WITH ELISABETH ROHM, THE ACTRESS BEHIND THE TROUBLED COP, TO LOOK BACK AT HER TIME ON THE SHOW, AND HER CAREER SINCE SHE HUNG UP HER LAPD BADGE…

In person at the BE Blowout convention, Elisabeth Rohm is warm, humorous, and gentle. However, she is often cast as tough-as-iron types: lawyers, stockbrokers, federal agents, and of course, *Angel*'s LAPD detective Kate Lockley.

Initially, Elisabeth says, she wasn't sure she wanted the part of Detective Lockley. "I auditioned for a really cool recurring role – short arc – and I liked it. It was this corrupt cop who had drug addictions. I auditioned for Joss Whedon and David Greenwalt and they offered it to me, and I said, 'Well, I've changed my mind, I don't think I really want to do it,' and Joss said, 'I want to talk to you philosophically and tell you about the show.' I was sitting on a beach in Malibu on the cell phone [talking to] him, and it kept getting static, but I heard him so clearly. He was one of the most brilliant people I'd ever talked to. He really is, to me, a media Dr. Seuss, someone who speaks in metaphor, who understands the deeper meanings of life and he knows how people will be able to comprehend them. You can't go up to somebody and say, 'These are my deep thoughts about the world.' You have to present it another way. A way they can actually hear it, and that's what Joss Whedon is really good at. He convinced me to do whatever I could do on the show, whether it was one episode or 10 episodes, because being on his show was so interesting."

Elisabeth, who was born in Germany but moved to the U.S. at a young age, was studying writing at Sarah Lawrence College when acting first became an option. "I liked to write and be in my own little world. It was peer pressure that made me get into acting, because the senior girls who lived in my dormitory in college were in the theatre department. I wanted their approval desperately, and I would try talking to them about acting. I started to audition for plays and it became a really cathartic thing for me. I had a lot of bravado when I was at a party, but I didn't necessarily have confidence from a deep place. Acting helped me develop that, because just to talk to people, to be warm and effervescent and kind, takes confidence. And

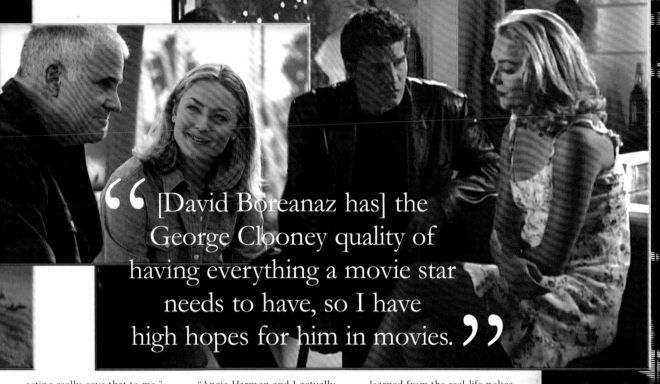

> **[David Boreanaz has] the George Clooney quality of having everything a movie star needs to have, so I have high hopes for him in movies.**

acting really gave that to me."

On graduating college, Elisabeth moved to New York City. "I decided to get a real job in the entertainment industry, instead of working [as a waitress] in a restaurant and going to auditions. I really wanted to understand how the industry worked, and what I needed to protect myself with – what kind of armor did I need to have in order to be tough enough to stand it all? So I got a job as an assistant to an agent, and I basically became a fly on the wall. I then went on to do a soap opera, *One Life to Live*, for six months."

When Elisabeth left the soap, she moved to Los Angeles. "I booked a leading role opposite Kyle MacLachlan in a TV pilot version of *The Invisible Man*. I think it was good. The show didn't get picked up, but Dick Wolf had produced it."

Wolf is perhaps best known for producing the *Law and Order* franchise. Although Elisabeth would become famous for her four years on *Law and Order* as Assistant District Attorney Serena Southerlyn, she didn't get cast on her first audition for the series.

"Angie Harmon and I actually screen-tested against each other. That was seven-and-a-half years ago; I looked like a baby, so Angie got it. She looked more sophisticated and serious. I rolled in with my Drew Barrymore cheeks and nobody really thought I was going to prosecute anyone – they thought I was on the way to a prom," Elisabeth laughs. "So that didn't work out. It was disappointing, but I did a bunch of different things, and then I got *Angel*."

Kate Lockley was Elisabeth's first role as a police officer, a job that led to a lot of real-life research. "[To play Kate] I studied with a SWAT team advisor, I learned how to shoot guns with the LAPD and I got into it. I wanted it to be gritty. I could [use] things that I'd learned from the cops [in the scenes]. I could say, 'Well, you don't know exactly where a predator is in the building, so don't walk in with the gun outstretched in your hands – kneel and crawl along the floor,' and different things that they had suggested that were dramatic."

The most important thing she

learned from the real-life police officers is, Elisabeth says, "They become their most calm in the scariest of situations, and that's what they're trained to do. It's not that they don't feel fear, but that they immediately know what to do with it. And they become their most steely, their most focused, and their most clear-headed, to accomplish what they need to accomplish."

Despite the intensity of many of Kate's scenes, Elisabeth remembers the *Angel* set as being a lot of fun, largely because of her fellow cast-members. "I became friends with David Boreanaz, Stephanie Romanov [Lilah Morgan], and Chris Kane [Lindsey McDonald]. I made good friends and became a better actor. I learned a lot from David. He's incredibly funny and he's gifted as a dramatic actor. I hadn't met anybody [prior to *Angel*] who was good at both. I always tell him he's Cary Grant – he's got the George Clooney quality of having everything a movie star needs to have, so I have high hopes for him in movies."

Sometimes, Elisabeth found it hard to keep a straight face. "David made me laugh, pretty

much incessantly, everyday. [He became] this Midwestern guy who'd be real wide-eyed, and he'd be investigating something, and he'd be like Norm [from *Cheers*]. He would pull this character out from time to time, and it was just the funniest thing."

In the original *Angel* pilot script Elisabeth read, Kate was a darker, drug-addicted character. She was made less tormented when she was first introduced in the series, but, Elisabeth observes, "It became darker for her, and they found their way back to her particular pain pretty quickly. It just wasn't being manifested so much as somebody who was undercover, somebody who kept getting involved in the darkness of what she was investigating. It was more that she had her own pain about her own childhood and towards her family and her father. Really, I think, there was a lot of love and companionship she felt from Angel, and unfortunately, when he [is revealed as a vampire], it's devastating for her. But in the beginning, I think she felt like she'd really found a friend, and she was pretty friendless."

As for Kate and Angel's relationship, Elisabeth says, "I [as Kate] expected things from Angel

and when I felt he couldn't come through for me, or he abandoned me, or pushed away from me because he knew he could never be what I wanted, that desertion and that abandonment was very painful, and eventually made me push against him. I wanted more and he could never have given me more, because he was stuck in his own personal hell."

Kate's relationship with her father Trevor Lockley, played by John Mahon, called for a different

> ❝ [Joss Whedon] was one of the most brilliant people I'd ever talked to. He... speaks in metaphor, [and] understands the deeper meanings of life. ❞

dynamic. "We had to really superficially bond, in a way, because we had to create a past with each other. So we would spend time with each other because we felt like we needed to be comfortable with each other. David and I could always be new – it could always be discovery, because there was the element of the unknown and we were not close to each other in the show. We could really, onscreen, learn who the other person was, so we were more in the moment. With the father figure, I had to create more of the past."

Elisabeth credits executive producers Joss Whedon and David Greenwalt with guiding her through how to deal with and how to play Kate's suicide attempt. "I talked to Joss and David about what suicide is – what that means and how you would play it – and they said to me, 'Look, when you are in that much pain, you're not howling at the moon – you've stopped howling at the moon. You're so tired. You're just done – you've got nothing left in you.' It's a very defeated feeling and their direction was not to overact it. That's what I kept writing on my script – 'I'm just so tired.' And I just walked in and did it. They

really led me to that – I don't know if I would have done that [otherwise]. I'm sure I would have walked in, I'd have been weeping and throwing things," she laughs, "but it was a very simple, bittersweet scene."

For Elisabeth, "The best and the hardest episode was ["The Prodigal"], when Kate found that her father had been killed by vampires. I literally started to hyperventilate. David was so good with me – he was like, 'It's okay, it's okay.' I was new in my career; that was the most emotional scene I had ever done, and it was devastating to play the thought of losing a father – how are you going to imagine your father dying? My father's still alive, but when you finally go there, it's a pretty devastating emotion – the person who you loved the most is gone. I felt it. And I was really in pain off-stage and David was stroking my back and helping me to breathe."

Given that her and David Boreanaz had a good rapport off screen, where does Elisabeth think the relationship between Kate and Angel might have gone? "Maybe if

I hadn't gotten *Bull* on TNT, I would've stayed and we would have discovered more of what happened, but I was offered my own show and so I left."

Bull, a show centered around the world of stockbrokers, only lasted 11 episodes, but three years after her original audition, Elisabeth was invited back to try out again for *Law and Order*. This time, she landed the gig, which lasted for four years.

Since leaving *Law and Order*, Elisabeth has starred in feature films *Miss Congeniality 2: Armed and Fabulous* – continuing her string of legal-related characters as an FBI agent – *Aftermath* and *Ghost Image*, and has also done an episode of ABC's *Masters of Sci-Fi*, and the telefilm *FBI Negotiator*.

Elisabeth is particularly proud of her work on the Lifetime Network movie *Amber's Story*, about the real-life origins of the Amber Alert, which notifies citizens when children have been kidnapped. "The producers were very passionate about it, and I said, 'Well, it sounds fascinating, I want this,' and they said, 'Okay, but you look nothing like [the real

Donna Whitson, Amber's mother] and you've never really proven to anybody that you will make those kinds of physical changes for a character.' So I got a documentary of [Donna]. She had dark brown hair to the middle of her back, wavy with bangs. She had a thick Texas accent, a very different background from me, a very different walk, a very different tone of pitch in her voice." However, Elisabeth pulled off the transformation for the role. "If you flipped through it [while channel-surfing], you wouldn't have even for a second thought it was me."

During her time on *Law and Order*, there was some discussion of Elisabeth revisiting *Angel* as Kate, but unfortunately, both shows filmed at the same time, and as Elisabeth was one of *Law's* leads, the scheduling could not be worked out. "We talked about it, but I was in New York. I would have flown myself out to work with David and work with my friends. I loved the show that much. It was one of the best experiences I've ever had as an actress, genuinely."

SHE'S ELEC

From the moment the sexy and sassy Gwen Raiden sauntered into the restaurant to deal with her latest client, Elliott, in the episode "Ground State," there was little doubt that actress Alexa Davalos and her cat burglar character would be adding a new energy to *Angel*.

"Oh my God!" exclaims Alexa. "We can all agree she's unlike any other character. The electrical power is just part of it. I thought, 'Wow! How fun would that be?' She also fascinated me because Gwen has this tough outer shell, and yet on the inside she's incredibly scared and insecure after growing up 'as a freak,' as she says. That duplicity of being very insecure on one hand and incredibly strong on the exterior is what attracted me."

Photo: Albert Ortega

It's all true. Although she's no slouch in the stealth department, Gwen is a walking conduit, capable of channelling and controlling electricity or discharging high voltage bursts. Those impressive powers can be deadly, so to fully understand their limitations, Alexa turned to the show's creative team for answers.

"There were parameters in which her powers lived by," explains Alexa. "The writers were helpful and I would say, 'You know, if I touch this, what happens?' They gave me an idea of what her physicality could be or not be. I had some freedom with it."

Due to the lack of control of her shocking abilities, Gwen was unable to come into direct contact with other living beings without severe, and possibly lethal, consequences. With other comic book references such as Electro Girl and Lex Luthor in "Ground State," Gwen's look-but-can't-touch policy was reminiscent of *The X-Men*'s Rogue, a young female character who faces a similar dilemma and who also wears gloves.

"I've heard this but I haven't seen *X-Men*," says the actress. "Part of me didn't want to see the movie when I was working on the show because I didn't want to have an external input, I wanted to do it on my own. Now that I'm not Gwen, I should really check it out."

Naturally, Alexa was slightly intimidated joining a cult

TRIC
C A I R N S

hit like *Angel*, but those nerves quickly dispersed as the friendly cast made her feel at ease. "They joke and they play," she says. "You have to remember – because they have been on the show for so long – they are a family. So when a newcomer enters, there's always an awkward beat. They were lovely, though."

Angel, Gunn, and Fred first encountered their formidable foe when both parties attempted to retrieve the extremely valuable Axis of Pythea. During their initial battle, Gwen strutted her stuff by almost killing Gunn and jump-starting Angel's undead heart. For Round Two, Gwen engaged Angel in hand-to-hand combat, a scene that had Alexa sweating buckets thanks to her unusually restricting attire.

"It was an absolute night-mare," she concedes. "The red leather pants were one thing, but the latex top was like wearing a balloon. It is incredibly hot to wear plastic, but it suited Gwen. It almost became comical at moments. I'm wearing these tight, unique pieces, and to choreograph the fights was very funny."

Gwen certainly made an impression on viewers, but the actress behind her wanted her to be considered more than just a souped-up thief. "Because she had this super power, which was so inhuman and something we can't relate to, it was a challenge to incorporate that into her and yet make Gwen feel like a real person," reflects Alexa. "I didn't want people to see her as this odd, alien-like woman without a sense of being human. She was very much a regular girl with this distinctly odd ability – and curse – in many ways."

Obviously, the writers had always intended on exploring Gwen's tortured history but even at the audition, Alexa reveals she was never privy to such information. "Well, not right away, any-ways," she corrects. "I knew I would be in an arc of some sort, and then I got the job and they started talking to me about the con-tract. I knew it would be for three episodes. There were discussions

of possibly more but I was doing another project so it got tangled."

Still, Gwen popped up two more times. In "Long Day's Journey," she came running to Team Angel after witnessing The Beast slaughtering one of her clients. However, it was Gwen's last appearance in "Players," where she enlists the help of Gunn for a mission, which proved to be the most entertaining for the actress. "The third episode I did most of my work with J., and we had so much fun it was hard to believe," she beams. "He's fan-tastic and I so adore him. We would sing between takes and do sit ups."

At the end of that adventure, Gwen obtained a device which would regulate her condition and allow her to touch other people. It appeared she and Gunn were about to hit the sheets together, and after breaking up with Fred, fans speculated this live wire had

Top Left: Alexa contemplates a difficult fight scene while having her hair and make-up fixed on *Angel*.

Above: Alexa co-starred with Hollywood action man Vin Diesel in *The Chronicles of Riddick*.

Below: Gwen set Angel's pulse racing (quite literally).

just stolen his heart. Despite the potential, Gwen was never seen again. "Unfortunately, the land of television is so fast and things happen so last minute that you have no way of being ready," explains Alexa. "When that chance came about, I was unavailable, which was sad because I would have loved to come back."

Instead, Alexa found herself in Vancouver shooting the big budget sci-fi sequel *The Chronicles of Riddick*. She eagerly embraced her role as Kyra, a tough-as-nails prisoner with a killer right hook and attitude, qualities that drew comparisons to Gwen.

"In both women, there is a young child buried beneath this habit of being strong, this survivor soldier quality," notes Alexa. "Kyra is literally a person who has traveled the galaxies, but emotionally there are similarities which I think there is with young women across the border. There's this sense of being invincible, and at the same time there's this innate

> The red leather pants were one thing, but the latex top was like wearing a balloon. It is incredibly hot to wear plastic, but it suited [Gwen].

THE BIG QUESTION

Angel's executive producer, Jeff Bell, gives his opinion on what happened between Gwen and Gunn

"The chemistry was definitely there. But our opinion was that it did *not* happen. It was just a big kiss. We talked a lot about that. I wasn't there, so I can't tell you for sure, but in terms of our intent, we don't think it happened. We always leave things like that open for question. It's better that way."

Photo: Albert Ortega

Above: Alexa and J. August Richards (*Angel*'s Gunn) get along off screen, as well as on. Photo: Albert Ortega

Right: Alexa stars in *Reunion*, a new show that traces the lives of six friends over the course of 20 years. Photo © Twentieth Century Fox

fear that comes from being a young woman."

With Alexa called upon to do some grueling elaborate sequences, she acknowledges that *Angel* proved to be a good training ground for such physical punishment. "To a certain degree, [the fact] that Gwen was this kick-ass who could fight and protect herself helped me," she says. "I had intense training for the *Chronicles of Riddick*, including wire work. It was good to have that little bit of experience but again, on television, you have about five minutes to learn that fight, where on *Riddick*, we had a lot more time. Any experience helps the next one, though."

Although she didn't know what to expect from her *Chronicles of Riddick* co-star, Alexa had nothing but praise for Vin Diesel. "Vin was so extraordinary to work with," she exclaims. "He is unbelievable. He was far easier than one would anticipate and he has an amazing imagination and passion. All of us actors could go to him and talk about the story and characters. He loved it."

Once again, Alexa proved to have the action chops, but with roles such as Gwen and Kyra in the bag, she could have fallen into that stereotype trap of being the new bad girl in Hollywood. "I

wasn't worried, but there were moments when I'd read a tremendous amount of scripts of that nature and I wondered what I would be doing for a while," she reveals. "On the other hand, I tried to find work that was different. I'd love to play as many different kinds of women as possible, yet I loved the sci-fi thing."

The CBS movie of the week, *Surrender Dorothy*, presented those new opportunities she was craving. Co-starring Academy Award winner Diane Keaton, the drama finds a mother coping with the sudden death of her daughter, Sara, played by Alexa. "Sara is a character unlike I've ever played in that she's a very, very, very normal girl going through normal things. No super powers and a little bit of inner turmoil, but not what I am used to. She's the girl next door with an edge."

At the time of this interview, Alexa was eagerly awaiting to see if her new Fox pilot *Reunion*, which follows the lives of six friends over 20 years, would be picked up for the Fall season, and now it has. "That will determine the next year of my life," she said. "It's an ensemble and we had an amazing time together."

Alexa sure has been busy, but then acting is in her blood. Both

her mother and grandfather were in the profession, and while she was a model in her early teens, she admits, "It was just something I did to help my family who were struggling back then. I always wanted to be an actress."

"[My mother] was very nurturing but terrified," explains Alexa. "To see your child voluntarily subject themselves to what this business truly is can be scary. But yeah, she really believes in me, which feels good."

After carving out a career in both television and feature film, no one is more surprised than Alexa to be returning to the small screen with so many projects. "To be perfectly honest with you, having a mother as an actress – who I watched struggle tremendously during my childhood – and to watch those fluctuations of ups and downs is difficult," she concludes. "She did mainly television, so I think I associated that with a life of inconsistency. As I've come into my own, I realize it has nothing to do with the medium. It has broadened my horizons in my own mind and ultimately it is about the character for me. If I read something and I fall in love with the character, no matter what it is, I'm eager to do it. That is what happened with Gwen." ✛

1986

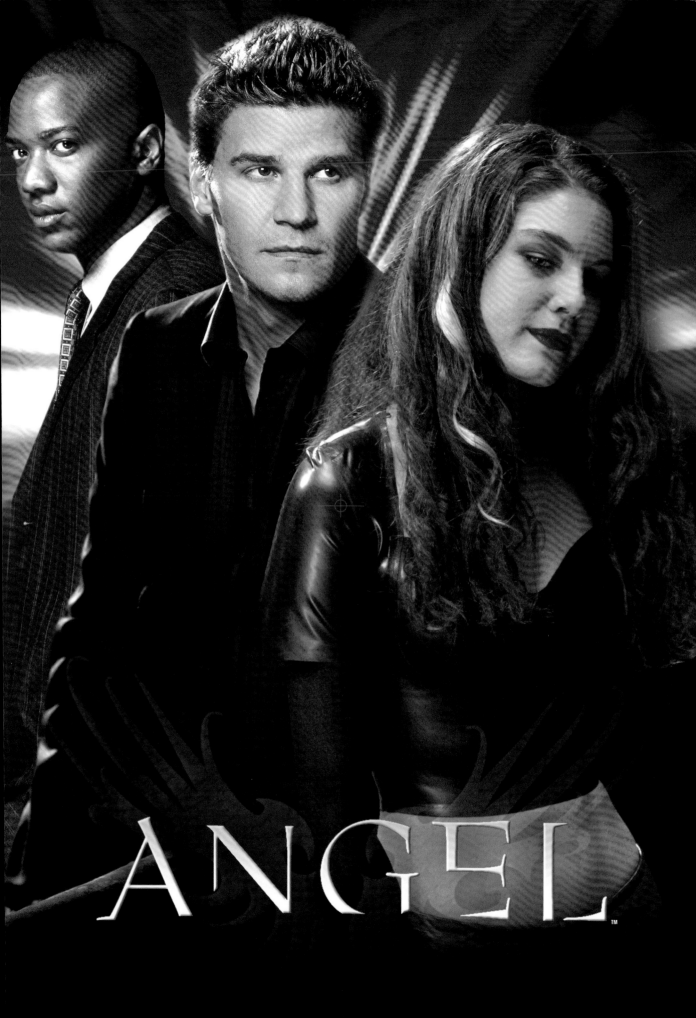

ANGEL™

STODDARD HAYES

ULTIMATE GUIDE TO ANGEL

THE COMPLETE LOWDOWN ON THE SERIES SO FAR...

I F YOU'RE NEW TO *ANGEL*, YOU'LL PROBABLY BE COMPLETELY BAFFLED AS TO WHY CORDELIA HAS A PHANTOM FLATMATE, WHY A GREEN-SKINNED KARAOKE-SINGING DEMON IS IN THE TEAM, AND WHY ON EARTH ANGEL KEEPS SINGING "MANDY" ALL THE TIME. BUT WE'RE HERE TO HELP WITH THAT IN OUR ULTIMATE GUIDE TO THE *ANGEL* SERIES SO FAR!

THE STORY SO FAR

SEASON ONE

ANGEL MOVES TO LOS ANGELES, where he joins forces with Cordelia and visionary half-demon Doyle, to open Angel Investigations, helpers of the helpless. While Angel befriends an undercover cop named Kate, Doyle dies a hero, but passes his visions to Cordelia. Rogue demon hunter Wesley takes Doyle's place and – surprise! – begins to earn his keep in their adventures. After several unfortunate encounters with Angel, the demonic law firm of Wolfram & Hart summon up his worst nightmare by resurrecting Darla.

BEST VILLAIN: The tag-team of Lilah and Lindsey start their joint career of fun, frolics and freaky mayhem.

HIGH POINTS: Cordelia gets a ghost for a roommate and almost has her eyes auctioned; a psycho stalker literally goes to pieces; Angel becomes a museum's best guide for two minutes and saves Faith's soul.

LOVE AMONG THE MONSTERS: Doyle has the hots for Cordy but doesn't have the nerve to ask her out; an actress hungry for immortality makes a move on Angel; and Angel and Buffy rekindle the flame when he becomes human for a day.

DEMON OF THE YEAR: Vocah. He brings back Darla, puts Cordy and Wesley in the hospital, and blows up Angel's 'batcave', providing the occasion for next year's move to the swanky Hyperion Hotel.

ANGELIC PROPHECY: Wesley deciphers a prophetic scroll which promises that after "the vampire with a soul" has fulfilled his destiny, he will become human again.

ALLEN FRANCIS DOYLE
PLAYED BY GLENN QUINN

Half-demon Doyle was sent to Angel by the Powers That Be, so that his visions could guide Angel to people who needed his help. Doyle had an unhappy lovelife, including a secret crush on Cordelia, and an ex-wife whose fiance tried to eat his brains. He served with Angel for only a few weeks before proving that he too was a hero, by sacrificing his life to save a group of half-demons from extermination.

LILAH MORGAN
PLAYED BY STEPHANIE ROMANOV

Ambitious, unscrupulous, and impossible to hate, Lilah has been involved in every kind of Wolfram & Hart mayhem, including torturing Cordy with evil visions, having

Drusilla sire Darla again, and sleeping with Wesley. When W&H was devastated by The Beast, Lilah took refuge at the Hyperion, only to be murdered by Cordelia. She now serves W&H in the afterlife.

LINDSEY McDONALD
PLAYED BY CHRISTIAN KANE

Lilah's chief rival at W&H, Lindsey sometimes disagreed with their methods. But that hasn't stopped him from being responsible for siccing Faith on Angel, bringing back Darla, and a few other good deeds. However, when W&H gave him an evil hand transplant, he realized he'd had enough, and left the firm and LA.

KATE LOCKLEY
PLAYED BY ELIZABETH ROHM

An undercover detective, Kate formed an alliance with Angel at first. But she was totally freaked to learn he is a vampire, and blamed him for her father's murder by vampires. She threatened to kill Angel when he protected Faith from arrest, and became so obsessed with the supernatural that she was fired from the police force. She tried to commit suicide, but Angel saved her – a turning point for both of them.

SEASON TWO

WOLFRAM & HART MAKE ANGEL have Darla daydreams to distract him from their nefarious plans. Angel tries to save Darla's soul, but when Dru turns her back into a vampire, he fires all his friends and goes solo to the dark side. He burns Dru and Darla, takes a tumble with Darla, then saves Kate, and finally returns to his friends, to ask if he can work for them. The whole gang takes a trip to Pylea, where Cordy becomes a princess and Angel becomes a beast, and rescues a missing 'cow' named Fred.

BEST VILLAIN: Darla goes from sultry siren to winsome dying waif, to crispy fried vampire, to mummy-to-be.

HIGH POINTS: Angel jousts on an L.A. boulevard and sings "Mandy"; Lindsey gets a demon hand; Numfar of the Deathwok Clan (a.k.a. Joss Whedon) dances up a

storm in Pylea; and Lorne loses his head, but not his voice.

LOVE AMONG THE MONSTERS: Wesley dates the cute and wealthy Virginia after saving her life; Angel has a final and fertile fling with Darla; Groosalugg hopes to live happily ever after with his Princess Cordelia

DEMON OF THE YEAR: Lorne. The swinging green demon Host has more style than even Angel – and he can sing a lot better, too.

ANGELIC PROPHECY: Lilah and Lindsey discover that Angel/Angelus will play a critical role in a major apocalypse, so he is no longer expendable to the firm – though they are.

ANGEL/ANGELUS

PLAYED BY DAVID BOREANAZ

AFTER THREE YEARS IN SUNNYDALE, Angel moved to Los Angeles to start his own detective agency and become a 'Champion' for the Powers That Be, and the chief adversary of the demonic law firm of Wolfram & Hart. He flirts with his dark side occasionally, first over Darla, then over the kidnapping of his infant son Connor, then over Connor's affair with 'auntie' Cordelia. Finally he goes head to head with Angelus in a drug-induced vision, which might finally lay the dark side to dust...

BEST KNOWN FOR being 'the Vampire with *Soul.*'

LIKES: Brooding; black leather dusters; Cordelia; Connor (well, most of the time); Barry Manilow.

DISLIKES: Wolfram & Hart, Angelus, bad guys of any species.

COOL LINE: LORNE: "Can't fight kyerumption, cinnamon buns. It's fate, it's the stars, kyerumption is—"
ANGEL: "Stop saying that! And stop calling me pastries!" ("Waiting in the Wings")

DARLA

PLAYED BY JULIE BENZ

Angel's sire, staked years ago, was resurrected in human form by Wolfram & Hart as a weapon against Angel. Angel tried to save her human life, but Drusilla sired her again to be a vampire, and Angel set her and Dru on fire. She slept with him hoping to turn him into Angelus, but instead conceived his child. The child's soul made her feel love again, and when she went into labour, she staked herself so that her child, Connor, would live.

DANIEL HOLTZ

PLAYED BY KEITH SZARABAJKA

The relentless vampire hunter of the 18th Century was transported to the present by a

demon, where he continued his quest to avenge Angelus' murder of his family. After kidnapping the infant Connor, he taught Connor to hate Angelus, then allowed the boy to return to his real father. His last act was to kill himself in a way that would convince Connor that Angel had murdered him, so that Connor would kill Angel and complete Holtz's revenge.

GWEN RAIDEN

PLAYED BY ALEXA DAVALOS

A self-described 'freak' whose body generates deadly electric charges, Gwen first crosses

paths with Angel and Gunn over the theft of an object of power, that both need. She joins forces with the gang in trying to thwart The Beast's plans to darken the sun, then later tricks Gunn into helping her steal a high tech device from an Asian crime lord, and uses the device to short out her electricity so she can experience touch at last.

CHARLES GUNN

PLAYED BY J. AUGUST RICHARDS

LEADER OF A STREET GANG of vampire and demon hunters, Gunn had to kill his own sister when she went vamp. Since leaving his gang to help Angel fight the good fight, he's had to learn that not all demons are evil and not all humans are good; he's also had to learn to get along with Wesley, whose feelings for Fred make Gunn as green as Lorne. His experience and street smarts make him much more than mere 'muscle'. His visit to the White Room at Wolfram & Hart may promise that a different role is in store for him...

BEST KNOWN FOR... being "the muscle" of Angel Investigations.

LIKES: Fred, big weapons, ballet.

DISLIKES: Vampires, rats, sometimes Wesley or Angel.

BEST LINE: "Damn, this is so much harder than it looks on *Batman!*" (fighting in "Ground State")

CORDELIA CHASE

PLAYED BY CHARISMA CARPENTER

CORDELIA ARRIVED IN LA AN unemployed actress, and quickly made herself Angel Investigations' office manager and bill collector. Since inheriting Doyle's visions, she has had an impressive supernatural career. She's been a Pylean Princess, a part-demon prophet, a Higher Power, and the mother of a Goddess. She also held the key to Angel's heart, until she started messing around with Connor instead. She was last seen in a supernatural coma, after giving birth to Jasmine.

BEST KNOWN FOR... being *the* bitch, whenever someone needs to be put in his (or its) place.

LIKES: Shopping, being a Princess, Angel, Connor.

DISLIKES: Visions, supernatural pregnancies, being a Higher Power.

COOL LINE: "God! I am *so* bored!!" (Higher Being Cordelia, "Deep Down").

SEASON THREE

A DEMON SPELL BRINGS VAMPIRE hunter Holtz to the 21st Century to seek revenge for Angelus' murder of his family. And some strange mojo brings Darla back to Angel, pregnant with his child. All the forces of evil hunt the miraculous mother and child, until Darla stakes herself to bring baby Connor into the world. Angel loves being a dad, but when Wes misreads a prophecy and kidnaps Connor, Holtz takes the baby into a hell dimension. A few weeks later, Connor and Holtz return to LA. Connor's now 16, an awesome demon fighter, and he's been raised to hate his real father, Angel – all part of Holtz' little plan for revenge, which ends with Holtz killing himself and Angel locked in a box at the bottom of the ocean.

WESLEY WYNDAM-PRYCE

PLAYED BY ALEXIS DENISON

ONCE AN INEPT WATCHER AND rogue demon hunter, Wesley has had a varied career with Angel Investigations. When Angel goes off the deep end over Darla, Wesley becomes the boss, until he misinterprets a prophecy, and kidnaps Angel's son Connor. Banished from Angel Investigations, he flirts with becoming a complete bad guy, and more than flirts with Lilah. He works his way back to the good by saving Angel from Connor's box and finding ways to fight The Beast – but still hangs on to the inner bad guy for emergencies.

BEST KNOWN FOR... scholarly knowledge of al things arcane and supernatural.

LIKES: Old books and weapons, Lilah, Fred.

DISLIKES: Holtz, Lilah Morgan, having his throat cut.

COOL LINE: "It's sad. The only way some people can find a purpose in life is by becoming obsessed with demons. By the way, Gunn, technically, that wasn't a Lurite, it was a Murite, a subspecies of the Lurite; the male sports a small, tell-tale fin just behind the third shoulder." ("Heartthrob")

BEST VILLAIN: Holtz. Even his supposed love for his adopted son takes second place to vengeance on Angel.

HIGH POINTS: Fred's parents help the Angel gang do a little bug hunting; everyone gets high on love at the ballet; Wes h a chat with a giant talking hamburger; an Holtz wipes the floor with Wolfram & Hart's thugs.

LOVE AMONG THE MONSTERS: Fred passes over fellow nerd Wesley to pair up with Gunn; Wesley jumps in the sack with Lilah; Cordelia and Angel miss out on thei chance at love when Cordy becomes a Higher Power.

DEMON OF THE YEAR: Skip. He's chatty, affable, loves *The Matrix*, and h the most bizzarro exoskeleton ever.

ANGELIC PROPHECY: On the day th pregnant Darla arrives, Fred and Wesle interpret a prophecy that says somethin is coming that will bring about the ruin tion of mankind.

DEMONIC PROPHECY: Demon SahJhan manipulates a prophecy so th Wesley believes Angel will kill Connor but the true prophecy says that Conno will kill SahJhan.

SEASON (FOUR)

WESLEY RESCUES ANGEL FROM THE deep, and Cordy returns from the Higher Plane, but not exactly in her right mind. First she sleeps with Connor, then she conceives a demonic child, then she starts talking in a booming male voice. The Angel gang brings back Angelus to fight The Beast, and Faith to fight Angelus, but they all end up fighting Connor, who keeps choosing the wrong side in the battle. Cordelia's radiant offspring, Jasmine, makes everyone into shiny, happy people for a little while, until Angel breaks her spell and Connor breaks her face.

BEST VILLAIN: Jasmine. She's the embodiment of love and peace – or would be, if she didn't wear live maggot face powder and snack on her worshippers.

HIGH POINTS: Fire rains down on L.A.; Wesley says goodbye to Lilah; Willow goes head-to-head with bad Cordy; Angel and his friends get the first class tour of their new facility, Wolfram & Hart.

LOVE AMONG THE MONSTERS: Connor and Cordy start a family; Fred and Gunn hit the rocks; Wes carries a torch for Lilah even though she's dead; Jasmine loves *everybody*, and everybody loves Jasmine. Well, almost everyone...

DEMON OF THE YEAR: The Beast darkens the sun over LA, conjures a rain of fire, and kicks the crap out of everyone. But he is just a minion…

ANGELIC PROPHECY: Remember those prophecies about Angel/Angelus having a role in a major apocalypse and Darla's offspring bringing the ruination of mankind? Hope you were paying attention. 🦇

WINIFRED (FRED) BURKLE

PLAYED BY AMY ACKER

ANGEL RESCUED FRED FROM A CAVE in Pylea, where she had been hiding from slavery. She has blossomed into an essential member of the team with her scientific expertise and her ability to kick butt while looking like a meek little nerd. She chooses Gunn's love over Wesley's, creating an awkward triangle, but her relationship with Gunn is rocked by guilt when she and Gunn take revenge on the professor who sent her to Pylea. She is the first to recognise Jasmine's true nature, and to discover how to free her friends from Jasmine's spell.

BEST KNOWN FOR… a scatterbrained but brilliant mind that makes Cordelia "look positively linear".

LIKES: Gunn, Wesley, math and physics.

DISLIKES: Pylea, interdimensional vortices, being betrayed.

COOL LINE: "Can I say something about destiny? Screw destiny! If this evil thing comes, we'll fight it and we'll keep fighting until we whup it. 'Cause destiny is just another word for inevitable. And nothing's inevitable as long as you stand up, look it in the eye and say, 'You're evitable!' Well, you catch my drift." ("Offspring")

CONNOR

PLAYED BY VINCENT KARTHEISER

CONNOR WAS RAISED AS HOLTZ'S adopted son in a Hell dimension, where he learned to be an awesome demon fighter, and to hate his real father, Angel. His miserable childhood has led him to betray Angel, get into a rivalry with Angel for the affections of Cordelia, and finally turn against all the people who care about him, for the sake of his and Cordelia's child. After Connor tries to kill himself and Cordelia, Angel makes a deal with Wolfram & Hart that gets Connor an entirely different, happy life.

BEST KNOWN FOR… incessant Oedipal rivalry with Angel.

LIKES: Cordelia, Holtz, tracking and fighting demons.

DISLIKES: Angel, magic, anything not human.

BEST LINE: "I know she's a lie – Jasmine. My whole life's been built on them. I just – I guess I thought this one was better than the others." ("Peace Out")

LORNE, AKA THE HOST, AKA KREVLORNSWATH OF THE DEATHWOK CLAN

PLAYED BY ANDY HALLETT

THE GREEN SINGING MACHINE LEFT his native Pylea because there was no music there. He is the owner and host of the demon nightclub Caritas until Angel and his friends burn the place down once too often. After his trip to Pylea reminds him why he left, Lorne moves to Vegas for a while, but returns to the Hyperion in time to be surrogate uncle to Connor, read people's minds at critical times, and offer warm fuzzies, supernatural advice, and cool music.

BEST KNOWN FOR… reading auras whenever someone sings.

LIKES: Music, Las Vegas, great clothes, cute nicknames.

DISLIKES: Pylea, having his nightclub set on fire, getting in fights of a physical kind.

COOL LINE: "This is way beyond my ken – and my Barbie and all my action figures!" (on first seeing the pregnant Darla, "Offspring")

EPISODE SPOTLIGHT

"SMILE TIME"

Original U.S. airdate: February 18, 2004

Synopsis

A popular children's TV show seems to be stealing the life forces of its young viewers by hypnotizing them. At the studio, Angel tries to discover for himself what evil source is behind the plan, but upon entering the building, he falls victim of a spell that transforms him into a puppet! It's left to Puppet Angel and the rest of the team to find a way to save the kids, reverse the spell and turn Puppet Angel back into his normal vampire state. In the meantime, an embarrassed Puppet Angel must also deal with werewolf girl Nina, who has returned and declares her romantic interest in the hunky brooding one. But she isn't aware of his recent, er… shrinkage.

Memorable Dialogue

Lorne: "Nina definitely wants a piece of Angel cake."

Fred: "Oh my God, Angel, you're cute!"
Angel: "Fred… don't."
Fred: "But… oh, look at your little hands!"
Angel: "You're fired."

Gunn: "You turned my boss into a frickin' puppet!"

Polo: "It's Smile Time!"
Angel: "No, it's time to kick your puppet ass all the way back to Hell."

Polo: "So, you got a little demon in you."
Angel: "I got a lot of demon in me."

Guest Star Info: Puppet Angel

Cute. Adorable. Sweet. Puppet Angel is David Boreanaz in miniature. Standing some 21-inches high, this wee little puppet man is an exact 1/2-scale version of the actual prop puppet seen in "Smile Time." Complete with spiky hair, faux leather coat, boots and trademark removable nose! Just to be spoilt for choice, there are three versions of this lovable little fellow. Following on from the original "Smile Time" Puppet, which sold out like hot cakes, Diamond Select has produced two more replica plush toys inspired by the fan-favorite episode. Battle Damaged Angel features slash marks on his face, while the soon-to-be-released Vampire Angel comes complete with fangs. Once again, each version is limited to a run of just 5,000. Getting your mitts on this replica plush is probably the closest most of us will ever come to getting a cuddle from the hunky, brooding one!

Statistics

 Number of times Puppet Angel gets embarrassed: a lot!

 Number of times Spike and Puppet Angel fight: 2

 Number of times Puppet Angel kicks ass: 1

 Number of puppets taken out: 4

 Number of kisses: 2

Trivia

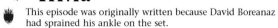

- This episode was originally written because David Boreanaz had sprained his ankle on the set.
- Joss Whedon had originally planned to direct this episode. But he decided to direct "A Hole in the World" instead.
- This was the first episode to air following the shocking news that the show would not be picked up for a sixth season.
- This episode was based on a story by Ben Edlund and Joss Whedon.

Compiled by Kate Anderson

Episode Credits

Written by:	Ben Edlund
Directed by:	Ben Edlund

Angel:	David Boreanaz
Spike:	James Marsters
Wesley Wyndam-Pryce:	Alexis Denisof
Charles Gunn:	J. August Richards
Winifred Burkle:	Amy Acker
Lorne:	Andy Hallett
Harmony:	Mercedes McNab
Knox:	Jonathan M. Woodward
Nina:	Jenny Mollen
Puppet Angel:	Drew Massey
Gregor Framkin:	David Fury
Tommy:	Ridge Canipe
Dr. Sparrow:	Marc Vann
Hannah:	Abigail Mavity
Tommy's mother:	Jennie Vaughn

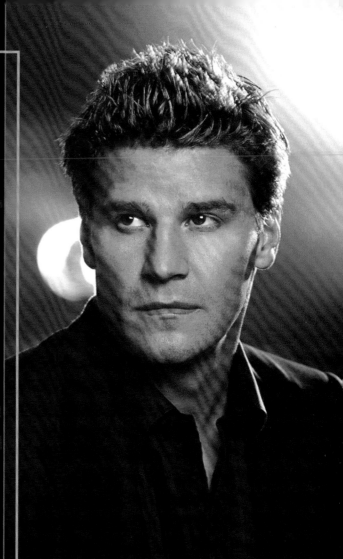

Part I

IT'S A WELL KNOWN FACT THAT WE NEVER KNOW WHAT GOES ON BEHIND CLOSED DOORS — BUT NOW WE'RE GOING TO GIVE YOU A CHANCE TO FIND OUT, IN A SPECIAL LOOK AT SOME OF OUR FAVORITE SETS FROM *BUFFY* AND *ANGEL* EPISODES GONE BY. OVER THE YEARS WE GOT GLIMPSES OF XANDER'S BASEMENT, CORDY'S BEAUTIFUL, IF SOMEWHAT HAUNTED, L.A. DES RES, AND ANGEL'S COMFY L.A. BACHELOR PAD — HOST TO HIS PERFECT DAY WITH BUFFY IN "I WILL REMEMBER YOU," BUT NOW WE EXPLORE THEM IN DEPTH. GET READY FOR SOME REVELATIONS, AS WE GO 'THROUGH THE KEYHOLE'!

Sets Appeal

Haunted House

O nly the best will do for Cordelia Chase, and her first apartment (9) was pretty far from it. Thanks to Doyle and a poltergeist who's willing to share its home with a still-breathing roommate, she's found just the spot to reflect her heightened tastes in L.A.

The high ceilings, arched doorways and chandelier of the living room (1) suggest a gothic Tex-Mex combination, while the dining room (4) aims for wholesomeness. The kitchen (2) does look a bit cramped, but it probably doesn't matter much to Cordy – she'd just as soon have a servant to take care of the cooking anyway!

Cordy's personal touch is all over the apartment, from the fashion magazines strewn about (7,5) to her prized beautifying tools (6) and a shelf full of awards (8), bittersweet reminders of her high school days.

When she wants a quiet retreat from the pressures of demonbusting, her conservative yet tasteful bedroom (3) provides plenty of peace. Unfortunately, with a poltergeist for a roommate, you can never truly be alone. It's hard to trust a locked door when there's a ghost floating about with abandon. ✤

Night Shift

O ne might think that after more than two centuries of investing, a guy like Angel would finally be able to retire. Then again, vampires have never been known for planning ahead. After all, it's not like they can bop around the islands playing shuffleboard in the sun. This season, Angel's keeping busy as an independent detective, which means he tries to help people he knows are in trouble without alerting the cops. He works out of his choice L.A. office (1, 5) with Cordelia and Doyle, and the trio seems pretty comfortable in this kind of noir setting. Hanging out with the Scooby gang – specifically a technophile like Willow – must have rubbed off on Cordelia as she modernized the place with a computer, multiple phone lines and a water cooler (2). The couch is probably Doyle's idea (3, 4) – it's perfect for sleeping off a rough night out. ✦

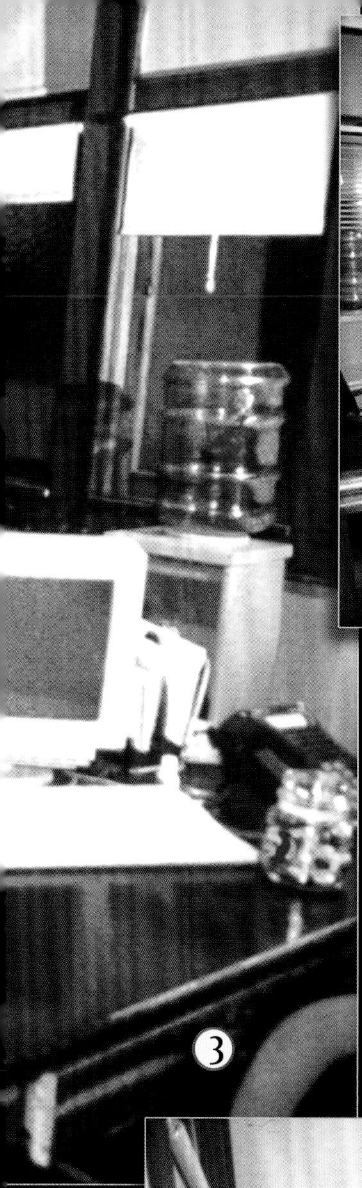
3

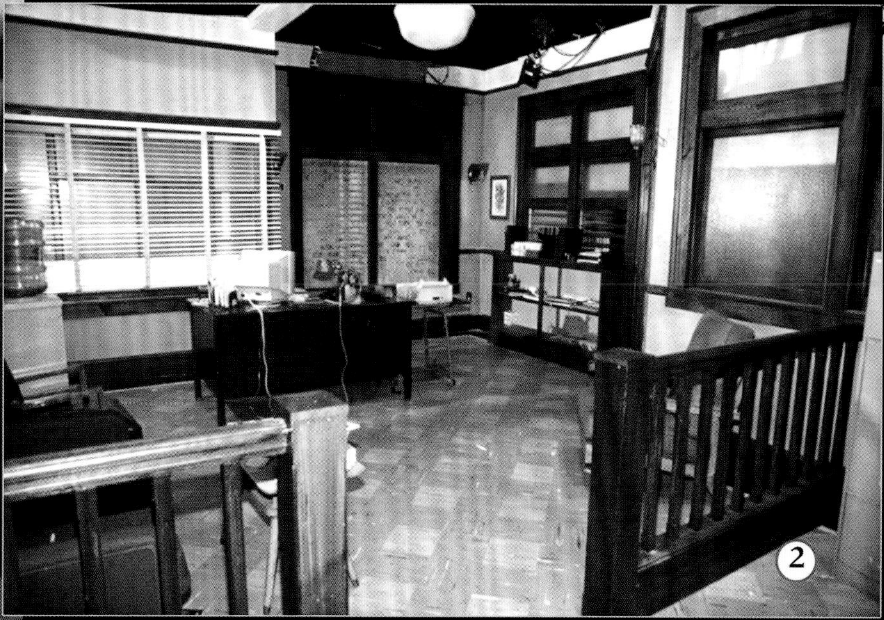
2

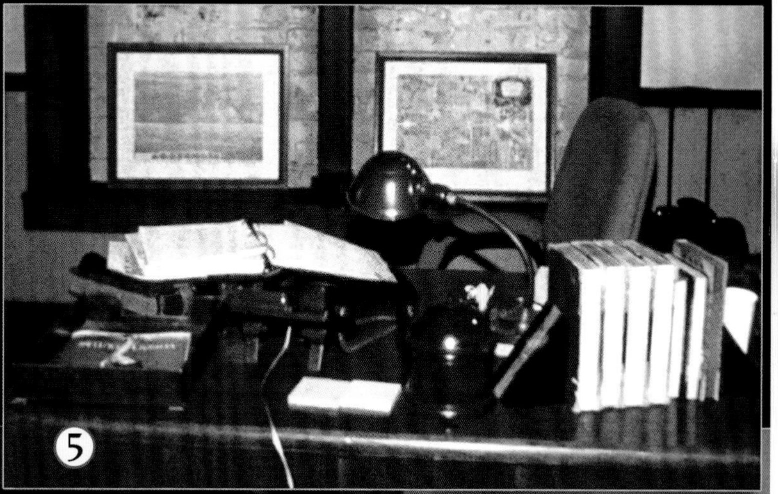
5

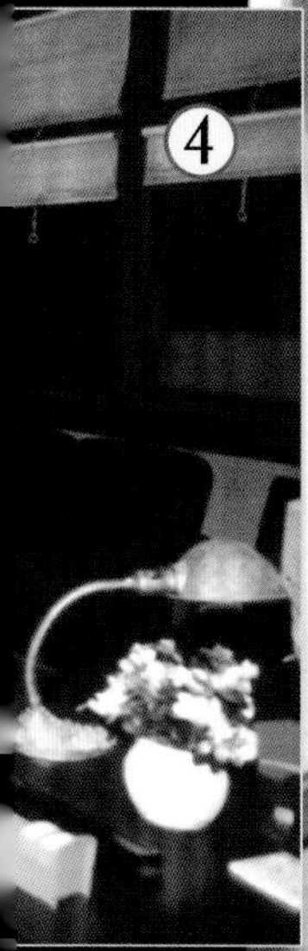
4

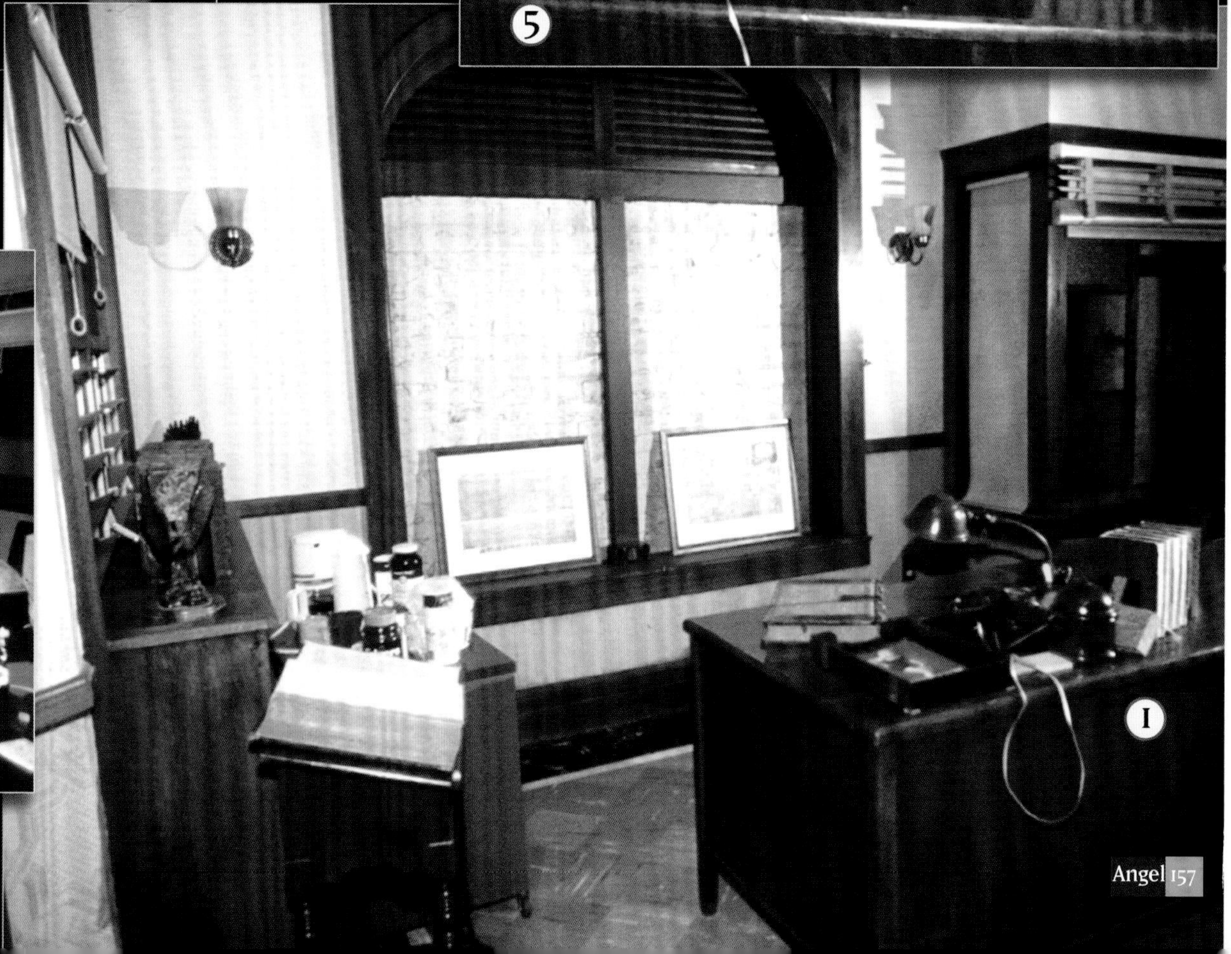
1

HALL PASS

Vampire
Lair

True Police

BIG CITY JUNGLE

CONFIDENTIAL
DETECTIVE
ANNUAL

The Bat Cave

I f all vampires had the same tastes as Angel (in decor, not blood), people would be lining up to get bit. Leaving his Sunnydale mansion behind, Angel has holed up in a tattered old building in Los Angeles. The place certainly has character, with a caged-in desk clerk (1) that accents the solitude of this basement fortress (2). It's the kind of location that allows Angel to hit the punching bag (3) and stockpile weapons (4) without raising an eyebrow from the neighbors.

Always one to be prepared, Angel's study (5) has vintage detective magazines (6) mixed in with countless tomes of spells, demons, and vampire histories. His living room has the ultimate lounge chair (7) in which to read or brood, and the creaky hardwood floors are a built-in alarm for intruders.

His bedroom is tucked away in a corner (8), and a private freight elevator (9) allows him easy access to and from the street to avoid meeting the neighbors. Vamps may have good taste, but nobody said they were personable. ✦

THE ANGEL ORACLE

BY ROB FRANCIS

SO YOU THINK YOU KNOW ALL THERE IS TO KNOW ABOUT ANGEL, DO YOU? NO? WELL, ACTUALLY, THAT DOESN'T SURPRISE US — BECAUSE THERE'S A LOT TO KNOW! IF THOSE GAPS IN YOUR ANGEL KNOWLEDGE HAVE BEEN KEEPING YOU AWAKE AT NIGHT, IF YOU JUST HAVE TO KNOW HOW ANGEL CAN BE PHOTOGRAPHED, OR EXACTLY WHAT THE RULES ARE FOR A VAMPIRE ENTERING A BUILDING, THEN YOU CAN REST EASY AT LAST. FORGET GIANT TALKING HAMBURGERS — IF YOU WANT ANSWERS TO ALL YOUR ANGEL QUESTIONS, THEN LOOK NO FURTHER!

KNOCK, KNOCK

File   Edit   View   Go   Bookmarks   Tools

CAN ANGEL BE INVITED INTO THE HOME OF A HUMAN BY A NON-RESIDENT OF THE HOUSE – HUMAN OR OTHERWISE?
No, otherwise Angel could just turn up at a place with, say, Gunn, be invited in by him and go wherever he likes. As the Season One episode, "Five By Five," demonstrated, this can't happen. It has to be a resident; otherwise it's strictly no entry until that person dies. If a family lived in the home a vampire wanted to gain access to, they'd all have to die before the vamp could just walk in.

SO HOW DID HARMONY GET INTO THE HYPERION HOTEL IN "DISHARMONY," THEN?
Hotels and other public buildings are usually fair game for vampires, as witnessed in the *Buffy* episode "Passion," when Angelus enters Sunnydale High School – without invitation – to kill Jenny Calendar. Even though Angel owns the Hyperion Hotel, it's a place of work where the 'helpless' (or should that be hopeless?) are always welcome, rather than a home that vampires cannot enter. And if anyone is pretty hopeless, surely it's Harmony?

Pretty much anything evil has been able to enter the Hyperion Hotel, except for the occasions when specific spells have been cast to keep things out.

What's far more baffling is the situation in Season Three's "Heartthrob," where Angel was unable to enter Fred's room without permission, even though it's part of the hotel. Fred may have made the hotel room her 'home' in a way, but that always struck us as a little odd.

WHY IS IT THAT IN "I'VE GOT YOU UNDER MY SKIN," AND "WHO ARE YOU?" ANGEL COULD ENTER A CHURCH? SURELY ALL THOSE CROSSES WOULD HAVE CAUSED HIM GRIEF?
It's not so much the building that's the problem but physical proximity to a cross. A vampire can stand pretty close to one and suffer bearable discomfort. Anything closer usually spells trouble. In Angel's parent show, *Buffy*, Spike found himself in a room packed with crosses, and was okay as long as he kept away from them.

ANGEL DUST

File   Edit   View   Go   Bookmarks   Tools   Help

WHY CAN'T YOU SEE A VAMPIRE IN A MIRROR, CAN VAMPS BE PHOTO-GRAPHED, AND WHY DO A STAKED VAMP'S CLOTHES TURN TO DUST, TOO?
Further to the *Buffy 101* feature, we came across this comment from Joss Whedon, which neatly explains all those nagging questions about vampire reflections/showing up on cameras etc. When asked why a vampire's clothes don't reflect in a mirror, Joss told the interviewer:

"It's the same reason their clothes turn to dust. They have a sort of aura; sort of the energy around them is affected by them. We had one line, and this is something that would have been useful, in the first season that had to be cut, which was when Buffy asked why Angel appeared on film when there are mirrors and cameras and what not. And it's simply, 'It's not physics, it's metaphysics.' And I was like, 'Oh my God, that's such a great line, it covers everything!'"

To add to this, although vampires shouldn't really make it into photographs as the focussing mechanism of most non-digital cameras involves the use of mirrors, they somehow always manage it on *Angel*. Our hero appears in a photograph from the 1950s in "Are You Now, Or Have You Ever Been?" and another during "Slouching Toward Bethlehem."

It's been argued by fans that digital cameras don't always use mirrors, and are therefore able to snap the undead. The same goes for video cameras, which are also capable of recording vampires.

WHY DOES ANGEL APPEAR IN THE SUN IN EARLY EPISODES OF THE SERIES?
Angel becomes immune to sunlight when continuity slip-ups occur during filming. This happened regularly during Season One, when light exposures to the film cameras were misjudged during early morning location shooting. The common excuse for these occasions is that Angel wasn't in 'direct' sunlight.

COULD A PERSON SIRED BY A SOULED VAMPIRE BECOME A GOOD VAMPIRE IN TURN?
Well, judging by what we've seen in the series, it doesn't look that likely. In "Why We Fight," Angel sires dying submarine crewmember Lawson in order to save him and the ship. When Lawson returns 60 years later, he hasn't exactly been leading a life of kindness to small blonde vampire slayers, as we can see from this exchange:

LAWSON: "I had this whole creature-of-the-night thing going for me – the joy of destruction and death – and I embraced it. I did all the terrible things a monster does – murdered women and children, tortured fathers and husbands just to hear 'em scream – and through it all... I felt nothing. 60 years of blood drying in my throat like ashes. So what do you think? Is it me, chief? Or does everyone you sired feel this way?"
ANGEL: "You're the only one I ever did this to... after I got a soul."
LAWSON: "Do I have one, too?"
ANGEL: "I don't think it works that way, son."

I think we can assume from that exchange that a vampire sired by a souled vampire doesn't get to keep theirs or have any greater capacity for good than a regular one. For example, Spike, even with a soul, still sired killer vamps in Season Seven, when he was under the control of The First.

IN ANGEL SEASON TWO'S "JUDGMENT," ANGEL BLEW OUT A CANDLE. BUT IT'S BEEN PROVED BEFORE THAT ANGEL HAS NO BREATH. WHAT GIVES?
Apart from the old excuse – sloppy continuity at the expense of great TV – our best guess is that vampires exhale something that is toxic to humans, making it unsafe for Angel to administer cardiopulmonary resuscitation (CPR) to Buffy. Vamps can clearly inhale and exhale something, as Spike's smoking has proved for several years (as does Angelus' killing of the smoking woman in "Innocence," for that matter).

DOES ANGEL'S HAIR GROW?
Yes. There aren't many obvious references to it in *Buffy* and *Angel*, but it's there if you read between the lines. For example, take a look at Spike in "Lessons." It's hard to tell if his hair is actually longer than usual, or just unkempt, but his roots are showing. That wouldn't happen if his hair didn't grow.

Also, Angel sets fire to Dru and Darla in "Redefinition," but Dru doesn't seem to have burnt or shorter hair in future appearances. We can only assume, therefore, that it grew back. We've also seen online references claiming Joss has actually stated that vampire hair does grow, although none of them point to a specific quote or interview, so we can't swear he definitely said that.

Done

BABY LOVE

File Edit View Go Bookmarks

WHAT WAS CONNOR ACTUALLY CREATED FOR?
Surely Connor was created to show teenage boys
how not to style their hair if they didn't want to
look like a girl? Seriously, Connor was designed as
part of the grand plan to bring Jasmine into this
world. In Season Five, the red demon – Cyvus Vail –
said he created Connor. However, he didn't mean
that he brought him into being to kill SahJhan. Vail
was referring to the work he did on behalf of
Wolfram & Hart to create a set of false memories for
Connor, that enabled the boy to believe he'd always
been part of a happy family. Connor was apparently
destined to kill SahJhan, but that was simply in addition to his mission to be Jasmine's dad. There were
probably a whole string of prophecies stating that
Connor was destined to do this, Angel was destined
to do that and Spike was destined to do the other
etc. They're creatures of many talents!

WHO PLAYED BABY CONNOR?
Baby Connor was played by a set of triplets, called
Jake, Trent, and (coincidentally) Connor Tupen. This
was their first Hollywood role. Union
rules don't allow babies to work on
set for any great length of time,
hence the need for more than one
infant. A dummy was used for shots
as and when the directors could get
away with it, too. Plastic babies tend
to be quieter and need changing a
lot less!

**WHAT HAPPENED TO CONNOR IN
THE SEASON FOUR FINALE OF
ANGEL?**
Angel persuaded Wolfram & Hart to
work their magic mojo and warp
reality – and people's memories – to
give Connor the proper family life he
missed out on due to Holtz and his
meddling in Season Three. It's a bit
like the situation with Dawn and the
monks over on *Buffy*, but with less
make-up and girly hair…

Done

TAT MAN

File Edit View Go Bookmarks

**WHAT ARE THE TATTOOS YOU CAN SEE ON ANGEL'S
WRISTS IN "ORPHEUS"? ARE THEY THE CHARACTER'S,
LIKE THE BIRD ON HIS BACK, OR DAVID BOREANAZ'?**
The only tattoo Angel is meant to have is the famous
gryphon perched on the letter 'A' between his shoulder
blades. David Boreanaz, however, has Kanji symbols tat-
tooed on the inside of both his wrists. Kanji symbols
originate in Japan, and appear to be an incredibly
complicated set of pictograms and icons used in body
art. We couldn't begin to tell you what David's translate
into, but there are several books and websites, such as
www.dsfy.com, if you'd like to explore Kanji more.
  Alyson Hannigan also has a Kanji tattoo on her
lower back, by the way. Not that we've looked.

Done

LOVE YOUR ACCENT

File Edit View Go Bookmarks

**WHERE IN ENGLAND DOES ALEXIS DENISOF
COME FROM?**
Just down the road from James Marsters in the little
village of Hollywoodshire. Seriously, Alexis was born in
Maryland, and raised in Seattle. After a stint at a
boarding school in New Hampshire, Alexis headed for
England in his late teens, where he spent the next 13
years perfecting his remarkable accent.
  You may have spotted him in several episodes of
Sean Bean's swashbuckling adventure, *Sharpe*, made dur-
ing that period. It's one of the reasons his English accent
is so good. Alexis returned to America after splitting with
his then-girlfriend, *Royle Family* and *Fast Show* actress
Caroline Aherne. The rest, as they say, is history.

Done

HOLLYW

24 CARITAS GOLD

File   Edit   View   Go   Bookmarks   Tools   Help

DOES LORNE'S BAR (CARITAS) JUST NOT CONDONE VIOLENCE, OR IS SOME MAGICAL MOJO STOPPING VIOLENCE FROM HAPPENING?
It's not simply because the clientele choose to be nice to one another. Caritas is protected from demon violence thanks to a Sanctorum spell cast by the Transuding Furies, three sisters seen in the episode "That Old Gang of Mine." The spell creates a mystical barrier that appears when violent demons try to attack someone in the club. "Transuding" means "to exude or give off." This may refer to the sisters' possession of some sort of mystical energy that they use to accomplish their work. The Furies returned in the episode "Dad," to place a protection spell around the Hyperion Hotel.

WHEN DID LORNE LOSE THE TIP OF HIS NOSE, AND WHY?
It's only natural to assume that Lorne didn't lose the tip of his nose in a fight, but embraced a great Hollywood tradition and "had a little work done." If you look a little weird, plastic surgery is just the thing to make a few improvements to what the gods of Pylea gave you.
    In reality, Lorne's make-up simply evolved over time, as make-up designer Dayne Johnson experimented with new and easier-to-apply prosthetics. Classic monster masks often change over the years, with the Klingons from *Star Trek*, Kryten from *Red Dwarf* and Davros from *Doctor Who* being some of the most heavily-remodeled cult creations. Even Angel's vamped-out look for "City Of…" bore little resemblance to that used on *Buffy*, but was altered back when the production team realized they didn't like the new look.

WHO ORIGINALLY SANG 'MANDY,' THE SONG ANGEL COVERED IN CARITAS?
Researching this just to be sure, we were surprised that the answer isn't quite what we were expecting. 'Mandy' was originally written and recorded by Scott English in 1971 as 'Brandy.' This version became a hit in the U.K. Barry Manilow subsequently covered 'Brandy,' but changed the name to 'Mandy' to avoid confusion with the Looking Glass hit 'Brandy (You're a Fine Girl)'.

WHAT IS THE NAME OF THE SONG PLAYED WHEN HARMONY WAKES UP AND GETS READY FOR WORK IN "HARM'S WAY"?
It's 'Hey Sailor' by The Detroit Cobras. It appears on the album *Life, Love And Leaving* LP/CD (Sympathy For The Record Industry, 2001, SFTRI 635).

WHO SANG THE SONG THAT FAITH DANCES TO IN THE SEASON ONE EPISODE "FIVE BY FIVE"?
Two tracks feature in the episode "Five by Five." The main track Faith dances to is a remix of 'Living Dead Girl' by Rob Zombie, from the album *American Made Music to Strip By*.

WHAT IS THE NAME OF THE TRACK YOU CAN HEAR IN "LONELY HEARTS" WHEN THE DEMON IS PASSING THROUGH ALL THOSE PEOPLE AND KATE IS TRACKING ANGEL?
It's 'Touched' by Vast, from the album *Visual Audio Sensory Theater*. You can find out more about the band (actually, it's just one guy – Jon Crosby) from the very cool Vast web site at www.realvast.com

Done

WIDE ANGEL

File   Edit   View   Go   Bookmarks

WHY IS THERE A MYSTERY GUY BEHIND THE COUNTER DURING THE CLIMAX OF "ARE YOU NOW OR HAVE YOU EVER BEEN?"
Good grief, you're absolutely right! We hadn't spotted that one before. It's an unwelcome by-product of the episodes being released on DVD in widescreen format when they were never meant to be seen that way. Although all episodes of *Angel* from Season Three onwards, and all *Buffy* episodes from Season Four and beyond, were shot using widescreen film and cameras, only Seasons Three to Five of *Angel* and the *Buffy* episode "Once More, With Feeling," were framed and edited by their directors with the intention of being broadcast that way.
    However, all the post-production work was carried out in widescreen, regardless of any quirky appearances by crewmembers on the edge of shot, and it was from these widescreen tapes that Fox produced the international versions of *Buffy* and *Angel* sent to overseas broadcasters. It was these master tapes that the *Angel* DVDs were made from.

Done

FANS FOR THE MEMORIES

File   Edit   View   Go   Bookmarks

WHAT'S THE ADDRESS OF THE OFFICIAL *ANGEL* FAN CLUB?
There are official fan clubs for both *Buffy* and *Angel*, run by VIP Fan Clubs.
Members receive:

- Gray "Wolfram & Hart Design" T-Shirt
- A special membership kit with official *Angel* merchandise and promotional items
- A 10 percent members-only discount on all official *Angel* merchandise
- Access to the exclusive *Angel* Fan Club Newsletter
- Access to limited edition members-only merchandise and special offers and promotions
- Goodies for sale from the *Angel* fan club include shooting scripts and Wolfram & Hart mugs, T-shirts etc.

VIP Fan Clubs also run officially sanctioned TV show auctions from E-Bay, which regularly feature props from *Angel* and *Buffy*. More at: members.ebay.com/ws2/eBayISAPI.dll?ViewUserPage&userid=vipfanclubs More details can be found at http://www.angelfanclub.com.

Done

LOCATION, LOCATION, LOCATION

File Edit View Go Bookmarks

WHERE WERE THE EXTERIORS FOR THE HYPERION HOTEL AND WOLFRAM & HART SHOT?

The Hyperion exteriors were filmed at the Los Altos Hotel & Apartments, located at 4121 Wilshire Blvd (on the north side of Wilshire, just east of Crenshaw Blvd.). Built back in 1925, they housed Hollywood stars such as Douglas Fairbanks, Bette Davis, Mae West, and Judy Garland. Wolfram & Hart is actually based at the Sony Pictures Plaza, opposite Sony Studios at 10202 W. Washington Blvd. That's on the east side of Madison Ave., between Washington Blvd and Culver Blvd in Culver City. By the way, the portal to Pylea, seen at the end of Season Two, is located by the front gates of Paramount Studios, where all the *Angel* interior scenes were filmed.

Done

UNALIVE AND KICKING

File Edit View Go Bookmarks

WHO SURVIVED THE FINALE OF "NOT FADE AWAY"?

Pretty much everyone, it seems. Because of all the recent attempts to get his TV movie made, Spike's in the clear, as is Illyria. She's expected to co-star in the movie. The IDW *Angel Old Friends* comics, sanctioned by Joss Whedon, see both Spike and Illyria, plus Angel and an eye-patch wearing Gunn, all still fit for duty – although it's not been stated for certain that this story takes place after the end of the show. With Harmony out of, er, harm's way before the classic alleyway showdown, as was Lorne, they're probably fine, too. And, of course, Cordy was long gone at this point. ✚

Done

Fang-

DESPITE
BEING BITTEN
DOWN IN ITS PRIME, *ANGEL*
STILL PROVIDED US WITH FIVE
FANTABULOUS
SEASONS. AND WE THOUGHT THERE
WOULD BE NO BETTER WAY TO PAY TRIBUTE TO
THE AWESOMENESS THAT IS *ANGEL*
THAN TO DEVISE OUR VERY OWN *ANGEL* AWARDS. SO,
THAT'S EXACTLY WHAT WE'VE DONE. EACH AND EVERY
SEASON WILL COMPETE IN CATEGORIES RANGING
FROM BEST EPISODE TO BEST SMOOCH, BEST
GUEST STAR AND MOST SHOCKING MOMENT...

tastic5

Season 1

Best onscreen chemistry: David Boreanaz and Sarah Michelle Gellar. They may now be in different shows, but they've still got the old magic.

Best special effect: Russell Winters burning up as he plummets from a skyscraper.

Most heroic act: Doyle gets yet another nod, for making the ultimate sacrifice for the greater good in, yes, "Hero"!

Most shocking moment: Couldn't be anything other than Doyle's death in "Hero."

Best smooch: Buffy and Angel locking lips in "I Will Remember You," closely followed by Cordelia and Doyle's smacker in "Hero."

Best overall episode: "I Will Remember You" because it sees Buffy and Angel reunited, living happily (albeit not ever after!) and being all lovey dovey with one another.

Best plot twist: The shocking death of Doyle. Hands up who saw that one coming?

Best exit: Doyle's heroic death in "Hero." It took the rest of the season, and then some, to recover.

Best kick-ass action scene: Tie between Angel kicking Russell Winters out of a high rise building – during daylight! – and the fight scene in "Somnambulist," where cop Kate stabs both Angel and Penn with a very large piece of wood.

Best use of music in an episode: Robert Kral for "Hero," with vocals by Elin Carlson.

Best villain: The Scourge. An army of Nazi-like pure-breed demons. Genuinely creepy.

Best hair & make-up: Tie between Doyle in demon form, and the Scourge.

Best writing in an episode: David Greenwalt and Jeannine Renshaw for "I Will Remember You." An emotional, intense, and beautiful episode that tugs at your heartstrings.

Best season guest star: James Marsters, because he made "In the Dark" one of the best ever episodes. Bai Ling as demon princess Jhiera in "She" gets a special mention because she was, well, cool.

Best supporting actor/actress: Charisma Carpenter, no contest! Buffy's loss is Angel's gain. Charisma steals EVERY scene that features the acid-tongued Cordelia Chase.

Best actor/actress: David Boreanaz. Gets his own show and proves that you can be drop dead gorgeous and still be a good actor!

Best overall episode: "Are You Now or Have You Ever Been." David Boreanaz acts his socks off in this unique look at Angel before he had a conscience. Simply unmissable.

Best actor/actress: David Boreanaz. He does his best acting to date in this season, taking Angel to the edge, and continues to prove that he was born to carry off lead duties.

Best supporting actor/actress: Alexis Denisof. Rugged and mature, the bumbling Watcher we used to know and love is no more. And that's no bad thing!

Best season guest star: Julie Benz. Whether playing Darla as human or vamp, Benz is awesome and has us feeling emotion we never felt possible for the sassy blonde.

Best writing in an episode: Tim Minear for "Are You Now or Have You Ever Been." Dark, dangerous and full of depth.

Best use of music in an episode: Christian Kane's beautiful *LA Song*, as seen in "Dead End."

Best hair & make-up: TV's coolest green dude, aka Lorne. Take that, Kermit!

Best plot twist: Wolfram & Hart bringing Darla back.

Best kick-ass action scene: Angel coolly and calmly setting Darla and Drusilla on fire in "Redefinition."

Best exit: Lindsey going out in style in "Dead End." From copping a feel of Lilah's behind, to firing shots at Wolfram & Hart big boss Nathan Reed.

Best villain: Lilah Morgan. Lawyers don't come more calculating and evil.

Best smooch: Any of Angel and Darla's lip-locking action. Take your pick!

Best onscreen chemistry: David Boreanaz and Christian Kane. The Angel/Lindsey dynamic came to the foreground and demonstrated the amazing onscreen rapport these two actors share.

Most shocking moment: Angel allowing Darla and Dru to feast on a room full of lawyers. And Angel sleeping with Darla.

Most heroic act: Angel saving a desperate Kate Lockley from committing suicide in "Epiphany."

Best special effect: Not so much a "special" effect, but we loved the slow motion effects in the scenes featuring the Fang Gang in China in "Darla."

Season 2

Best overall episode: "Birthday." This episode alone really shows Cordelia's character growth. Plus the alternate reality sequence and Doyle, albeit in flashback, are an extra treat.

Best actor/actress: Alexis Denisof. Wesley undergoes a complex journey from a rational, intelligent and dependable man at the beginning, to a desperate, conflicted wreck of a man on the verge of self-destruction at the end.

Best season guest star: Keith Szarabajka as Daniel Holtz. He managed to make us have some compassion for what should have been a thoroughly unlikable character on paper.

Best writing in an episode: "Waiting in the Wings." A perfect showcase for the talent that is Joss Whedon. This episode demonstrates Whedon's incredible ability to tell a good story.

Best use of music in an episode: Marti Noxon for Cordelia's TV show theme in "Birthday." It's sooo Cordy!

Best hair & make-up: We thought the gang have never looked more spiffing than in their evening-wear in "Waiting in the Wings."

Best plot twist: Darla pregnant with Angel's baby and Connor returning as a teenager out for revenge on Angel.

Best kick-ass action scene: A revenge-fueled Connor taking on Angel, Groo and Gunn in "A New World."

Best exit: Darla, for staking herself so that her unborn baby could live. There's no greater act of love than self-sacrifice.

Best smooch: Angel and Cordelia snogging rather a lot in "Waiting in the Wings." Who cares that they were possessed, it's hot stuff!

Best onscreen chemistry: David Boreanaz and Julie Benz.

Most shocking moment: Wesley kidnapping Connor. His betrayal and subsequent exile was shocking.

Most heroic act: Cordelia giving up her dreams of stardom to save Angel's sanity and become part-demon in the process.

Best special effect: In "Loyalty," *THAT* talking hamburger!

Best supporting actor/actress: Stephanie Romanov for a remarkable turn as evil lawyer Lilah Morgan. The character finally reaches her full egotistical, heartless, and sarcastic potential. Almost as heartless as a soulless Angelus.

Best villain: Daniel Holtz. Ruthless and manipulative, Holtz was a quietly underplayed, emotionally powerful character, full of complexity and driven by a lust for revenge.

Season 3

Season 4

Best writing in an episode: "Spin the Bottle." Team Angel as teenagers. Inspired. Hilarious. And it's written by Joss. What more could we ask for?!

Best use of music in an episode: *Wouldn't It Be Nice* by The Beach Boys, as heard in "The Magic Bullet."

Best hair & make-up: That would be The Beast.

Best plot twist: The return of Angelus. Definitely the highlight of a very dark season.

Best kick-ass action scene: The Beast tossing everyone around like rag dolls in "Apocalypse, Nowish."

Best exit: Lilah's death. Not once, but twice. Stabbed by Cordelia and then beheaded by Wesley.

Best overall episode: "Orpheus," because it's full of twists and turns. There's Willow; Angelus vs. Angel; and Faith willing to go not only to the edge, but over it, in order to save Angel.

Best actor/actress: David Boreanaz, who more than rose to the challenge of playing the many facets to his character, whether it be troubled father, potential lover, or evil vampire.

Best supporting actor/actress: Vincent Kartheiser as Connor. His hooking up with Cordy didn't go down well. But Kartheiser rose to the challenge admirably and, by the end of the season, we realized that there was more to him that just an angry, unsympathetic teenager.

Best season guest star: Alexa Davalos as the mutant girl with destructive electrical powers, Gwen Raiden, introduced in "Ground State."

Best villain: Jasmine. Her twisted ideology of a constructed peace, which would see the sacrifice of thousands for the benefit of millions wasn't actually all that twisted after all. A unique Big Bad.

Best smooch: Gwen and Gunn's kiss from "Players."

Best onscreen chemistry: Lilah and Wes. We shouldn't really have loved them together quite as much as we did.

Most shocking moment: Not so much a moment, but seeing Wesley and Lilah *AND* Cordelia and Connor getting it on was the most shocking thing about Season Four!

Most heroic act: Gunn stepping in and saving Fred from doing the unthinkable and killing Professor Seidel in "Supersymmetry" – only to do the job himself!

Best special effect: The Apocalypse falling down upon Los Angeles.

Best plot twist: Angel and the gang getting to run Wolfram & Hart. Oh, and we can't overlook the return of Spike!

Season 5

Best exit: Goes to the whole of Team Angel. They went out in style: fighting the good fight.

Best overall episode: "You're Welcome." Cordy returning to steer Angel back on track is a perfectly fitting "goodbye" for such a legendary character.

Best actor/actress: Amy Acker. If Fred's death scene wasn't enough of an example of Acker's acting skills, then her turn as the confused and angry ex-goddess Illyria most certainly was.

Best kick-ass action scene: Spike and Angel's slugfest in "Destiny." It's the culmination of their centuries-old conflict, complete with some good old-fashioned fisticuffs and brilliant banter.

Best villain: The Circle of the Black Thorn from "Power Play." Not the kind of circle you'd want to play pass-the-parcel with, that's for sure!

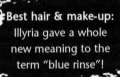

Best hair & make-up: Illyria gave a whole new meaning to the term "blue rinse"!

Best smooch: Angel and Cordy's smacker in "You're Welcome."

Best onscreen chemistry: Alexis Denisof and Amy Acker were outstanding in all of their Wes/Fred moments.

Most shocking moment: Slayer Dana chopping off Spike's hands; Wesley's death; the realization that Cordelia never actually came out of her coma; and Fred's transformation into Illyria.

Most heroic act: A broken Lorne, doing the completely unthinkable and killing Lindsey; not for his sake but for Angel and the greater good.

Best special effect: The army of demons (including the 100-foot tall giant and flying dragon!) at the close of "Not Fade Away." ✛

Best supporting actor/actress: James Marsters. Watching Spike continue to explore his journey towards redemption brought a whole new dimension to the show.

Best writing in an episode: "Smile Time." Just as Buffy did with "Hush" and "Once More, With Feeling," *Angel* gets to play outside the box. Dark and disturbing, but also thought-provoking and hilarious.

Best use of music in an episode: "A Place Called Home" by singer/song-writer, Kim Richey, as seen in the end montage in "Shells."

Best season guest star: Charisma Carpenter, although Carole Raphaelle Davis as the over-the-top head of the Italian branch of W&H and Puppet Angel were close contenders.

CLASSIC SCENE

"NOT fade AWAY"

"I kind of want to slay the dragon."

The Story so far...

Angel and the gang prepare to bring down the Circle of the Black Thorn. Determined to go out fighting, Angel faces off against Hamilton, the Senior Partners' henchman, Spike confronts a demon cult, Lorne takes out Lindsey, Gunn takes on an evil senator, and Wes confronts the wicked sorcerer, Cyvus Vail.

The Scene...

AN ALLEY BEHIND THE HYPERION HOTEL, LOS ANGELES, AT NIGHT.
(Angel rendezvous in an alley with the surviving members of Team Angel. It's night, the rain is pouring down, and this could be their final ever battle...)

SPIKE: (Out of shot.) Boo. (He walks out of the shadows.)

ANGEL: Anyone else?

SPIKE: Not so far. You feel the heat?

ANGEL: It's coming.

SPIKE: Finally got ourselves a decent brawl. (Gunn appears, running toward them.)

GUNN: Damn! How did I know the fang boys would pull through?

(As Gunn gets closer, his steps become progressively weaker.)

GUNN: You're lucky we're on the same side, dogs, 'cause I was on fire tonight. (Weakly.) My game was tight.

(Gunn almost collapses, but Angel and Spike catch him. They help him to a box so he can sit down.)

SPIKE: (Looking at Gunn's wounds.) You're supposed to wear the red stuff on the inside, Charlie boy.

GUNN: (Looks at his wounds.) Any word on Wes?

ILLYRIA: (Jumping down from the chain-link fence.) Wesley's dead.

(Angel looks heartbroken by the news; Gunn bursts into tears and Spike hangs his head.)

ILLYRIA: I'm feeling grief for him. I can't seem to control it. I wish to do more violence.

SPIKE: (A crowd clamors in the background.) Well, wishes just happen to be horses today.

ANGEL: Among other things.

(Angel looks at the approaching crowd of hundreds, if not thousands, of demons, all different sorts, shapes and sizes. A huge dragon flies towards them overhead.)

GUNN: OK. You take the 30,000 on the left...

ILLYRIA: You're fading. You'll last 10 minutes at best.

GUNN: (Standing.) Then let's make 'em memorable.

(Angel steps forward and Spike, Gunn and Illyria follow. They stare at the hordes of approaching demons.)

SPIKE: In terms of a plan?

ANGEL: We fight.

SPIKE: Bit more specific.

ANGEL: (Stepping forward.) Well, personally, I kind of want to slay the dragon. (The demons begin their attack.) Let's go to work. (Swinging his sword.) (Fade to black.)

EPISODE CREDITS

Season Five, Episode 22

first aired: 19/05/04 (US) & 08/06/04 (UK)
written by: Jeffrey Bell & Joss Whedon
directed by: Jeffrey Bell
Main actors this scene:
Angel: David Boreanaz
Spike: James Marsters
Gunn: J August Richards
Illyria: Amy Acker

WHY SO COOL?

Heart-rending and deeply unsettling, this final scene is nonetheless a fitting denouement for the show. And while the series may be no more (sob), at least it didn't fade away; it went out in style, at the top of its game. Plus it's kinda cool to think that Team Angel is still out there, somewhere, fighting that dragon.

EPISODE TRIVIA

 After the episode aired, as a thank-you to all its loyal viewers, The WB network played a montage of scenes from the show's history.

 Ratings for *Angel*'s season finale actually beat *Buffy*'s season finale.

Compiled by Kate Anderson

OTHER GREAT TV TIE-IN COMPANIONS FROM TITAN

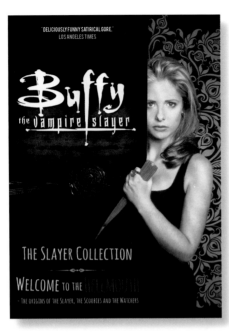

Buffy - The Slayer Collection: Welcome to the Hellmouth
On sale November 2015
ISBN 9781782763642

The X-Files - The Official Collection Volume 1
On sale January 2016
ISBN 9781782763710

COMING SOON...

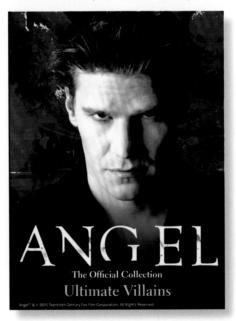

The Official Collection Volume 2 - Ultimate Villains
On sale May 2016
ISBN 9781782763697

For more information visit www.titan-comics.com

TITANCOMICS